PRAISE FOR *FULFILL YOUR STUDENT MINISTRY*

"As dean of Spurgeon College at Midwestern Seminary, Sam Bierig is on the cutting edge of student ministry in North America. *Fulfill Your Student Ministry: A Manifesto and Field Guide* is the first fruits of Bierig's, and his coauthors', work. In these pages you'll find instruction that is biblically faithful and practically helpful. I highly recommend this book to all who are engaged with students, either as parents, teachers, or ministers."

Jason K. Allen, Ph.D., author of *Being a Christian: How Jesus Redeems All of Life*
President and Professor of Preaching and Pastoral Ministry
Midwestern Baptist Theological Seminary & Spurgeon College

"If you want the antidote to what ails evangelicalism's student-ministry culture, including the long-lamented 70 percent dropout rate for young adults, you will find it in this book. Sam Bierig and company have compiled a step-by-step guide to returning youth to the only sources of power and wisdom for joy and growth in Christ. Take heed."

Jared C. Wilson, author of *The Gospel-Driven Church*
Assistant Professor of Pastoral Ministry
Midwestern Baptist Theological Seminary & Spurgeon College

"As a parent of teenagers, I am focused more than ever before on the state of student ministry. As someone who helps train future church leaders, I've been around many student ministers and know that there has long been a need for a book like this. I'm grateful that this book has arrived at this time to speak to these issues. More than that, I admire these authors and church leaders for what they've written. Read this book and share it. Parents like me will thank you."

Jason G. Duesing, Ph.D., author of *Mere Hope: Life in An Age of Cynicism*
Provost and Associate Professor of Historical Theology
Midwestern Baptist Theological Seminary & Spurgeon College

FULFILL YOUR STUDENT MINISTRY

A MANIFESTO AND FIELD GUIDE

Samuel L. Bierig

Contributors: Rechab Gray, H. Jared Bumpers, Samuel L. Bierig, Royland Kirkwood, David Bronson, Joel Muddamalle, Joel Cowart

Fulfill Your Student Ministry: A Manifesto and Field Guide

ISBN 978-1-948022-15-6

Rainer Publishing
www.RainerPublishing.com
Spring Hill, TN

Printed in the United States of America

FOREWORD

I am the product of a church that took student ministry seriously.

My father's congregation was not large. The church did not have the financial resources, meeting space, or paid staff to pull off youth ministry with a wow factor. Everything we did was low-tech. But the Lord saved me, called me to preach, and set me on the path to faithful discipleship and fruitful ministry through the brothers and sisters who ministered to the young people of our church.

That wonderful congregation taught me devotion to Christ, the power of prayer, the wisdom of Scripture, the importance of holiness, a lifestyle of service, a commitment to the church, and a burden for the lost. So what if we didn't have a lot of bells and whistles?! My life and ministry are the fruit of leaders who fulfilled their student ministry.

Youth ministry should be fun. Students should want to participate. It is great when young people are dragging their parents to attend, not the other way around. But if the attraction of your student ministry is primarily about fun and games, you will attract crowds without making disciples. The Great Commission also applies to student ministry (Matt 28:18–10). The mission is to make disciples of the Lord Jesus Christ. The gospel should be preached to young people to lead this to saving faith in Christ, and the Word of God should be taught to young people to help them to trust and obey the lordship of Christ over their lives.

Student ministry dedicated to making disciples is spiritual warfare. The enemy of our souls is determined to win over our young people to the sinful things of this world (1 John 2:15–17). We must be all the more determined to reach the students under our charge with the gospel of Jesus Christ. *Fulfill Your Student Ministry* is a spiritual battle plan to help student ministry leaders fight the good fight as they serve youth and families in the local church.

A focus on church-growth techniques has seduced many congregations to be preoccupied with results. The wrong kind of results—numerical success without spiritual impact. This foolish embrace of pragmatism has ruined the health of many congregations. But the consequences on students have been even more severe. Preoccupation with results leads congregations down the wrong path. And it typically leads young people out of the church. In contrast, *Fulfill Your Student Ministry* offers a Christ-centered,

Bible-based, gospel-saturated philosophy of student ministry. It is written by men in the trenches, not mere theorists. With an unwavering commitment to Christ and the church, these student pastors share principles and practices for developing a biblically faithful and spiritual fruitful student ministry.

The beloved deacon chairman in my father's church would often say the young people of the congregation were the locomotive, while he and my father were the caboose. They were where the church had been. We were where the church was going. The same is true of the young people in your congregation. In a real sense, *Fulfill Your Students Ministry* sets the tracks to ensure your student ministry is headed in the right direction. Read it. Share it widely in your church. Implement its strategies in student ministry. And trust the Lord to give the increase!

H.B. Charles Jr.
Shiloh Church
Jacksonville, Florida

CONTENTS

Introduction (Samuel Bierig) 11
Chapter 1: Student Ministry, the Bible, and the Gospel (Rechab Gray) 17
Chapter 2: Student Ministry, The Bible, and the Local Church (H. Jared Bumpers) 31
Chapter 3: Student Ministry, the Bible, and Discipleship (Samuel Bierig) 45
Chapter 4: Student Ministry, the Bible, and Preaching (Royland Kirkwood) 61
Chapter 5: Student Ministry, the Bible, and Worship (David Bronson) 73
Chapter 6: Student Ministry, the Bible, and Sexual Holiness (Samuel Bierig) 87
Chapter 7: Student Ministry, the Bible, and Mission Trip (H. Jared Bumpers) 105
Chapter 8: Student Ministry, the Bible, and Parents (Rechab Gray) 117
Chapter 9: Student Ministry, the Bible, and Multi-Ethnicity (Joel Muddamalle) 127
Chapter 10: Student Ministry, the Bible, and Evangelism (Joel Cowart) 141

INTRODUCTION

Sam Bierig

Student ministry is in a bad way. But you already knew that, didn't you? I could start out by turning a fire hose of depressing statistics on you like, "The first 300 out of every 200 students that graduate out of your student ministry will fall away from the church by Thursday of their third week in college. Did you know that, *student pastor*? . . . *DID YOU EVEN KNOW THAT??*" We've all heard those stats and their accompanying pep talks. I've never found them to be all that helpful or motivating, frankly. I suspect you haven't either. The fact that you picked up this little book tells me you sense something isn't quite right about student ministry, and you don't need some guy Gatling gunning a bunch of stats at you until your eyes flip back into your head to figure it out. You know something has gone wrong, but you can't quite put your finger on it. Or, maybe you have put your finger on it, but you need some confirmation.

I cut my teeth in the pastorate by way of student ministry way back circa 2005. Student ministry was a mess back then, and it's still a mess—but it's a mess the contributors of this book feel has value and remains worth tidying up. We love student pastors, and we love student ministry. We write with hearts burdened by that love. We don't think student ministry should be thrown away, and we have great hope for its future. Now, allow me to introduce you to your squad of student pastor-theologians!

Dr. Jared Bumpers. Jared has served in student ministry for over eleven years and has another two years of serving as a teaching pastor under his belt. He is currently the director of student life and events at Spurgeon College and Midwestern Baptist Theological Seminary in Kansas City, MO. Jared wrote the chapters on the local church and short-term student mission trips. And just so you know the kind of guy you are dealing with, Jared once ripped his ring finger off his hand at a lock-in while playing capture the flag! I don't really know what else you need to know about Jared to trust that he can speak authoritatively on our subject. *Hard core much, Jared?* Wowza!

Rechab Gray. Rechab has served in student ministry for over seven years, most of which was in Philadelphia at Epiphany Fellowship. Rechab wrote the chapters on the gospel and navigating the waters of parents and student ministry. He now lives in Des Moines, IA, and serves as one of the teaching pastors at Cottage Grove Church. Rechab once took a group of high school students through a McDonalds drive thru but failed to give precise direction on how to order. Big mistake, Rechab. A couple of the high school guys proceeded to ask the McDonalds worker for her cell number. Neither Rechab nor I can confirm whether his students actually got the cell number!

Joel Muddamalle. Joel served in student ministry for nine years before taking up his current post as director of theology at Proverbs 31 Ministries. He wrote the chapter on pursuing multi-ethnic student ministries. While leading a junior high canoeing trip, Joel once came face-to-face with a bear. At first, he thought it was just one of the junior high kids pulling a prank, but when he walked out of his tent he was looking Smoky the Bear square in the eyes. Joel did what you would do: he ran away, leaving his little junior high flock completely defenseless. It's okay, Joel, we forgive you. You are a model for student pastors everywhere. No *junior high students were hurt in the making of this true story!*

Joel Cowart. Joel has served in both college and student ministry for going on nine years now. He currently serves as pastor of young Adults at Shiloh Metropolitan Baptist Church in Jacksonville, FL. Joel doesn't really have any cool student ministry stories—or so he says. But he is a vegan, which makes for a really sad life in my estimation. Folks, that means he doesn't ever eat meat. Ever! But you should know that even though he doesn't eat meat, he is an absolutely carnivorous evangelist. And because he has an all-consuming passion for sharing the gospel with the lost, it is appropriate that he supplies us with the chapter on evangelism.

Royland Kirkwood. Roy has served in student ministry for over eleven years now. He currently serves as one of the Student Pastors at Shiloh Metropolitan Baptist Church in Jacksonville, FL. He wrote the chapter on student ministry and preaching. Roy, while running from a student at a student lock-in, nearly broke his leg by running into a wall. But being the tough guy Roy is, he chose not to go to the ER lest the senior pastor figure out he and the student were actually running through parts of the church they were told to avoid. Wise guy . . . I think.

David Bronson. He has over seven years of student ministry experience in both rural and urban contexts. He currently serves as a pastor at Liberty Baptist Church in Liberty, MO. David once chugged a 20-ounce bottle of syrup at a youth event. He promptly hurled all 20 ounces, which provided just the sermon illustrated needed. Pretty legit dude, I'd say. He'll be covering the chapter on worship.

Last, there's me. Sam Bierig. I serve as the dean of Spurgeon College in Kansas City, MO. Besides this introduction, I wrote the chapters on discipleship and dating (sexual holiness). Lucky me. As for cool stories, there are a lot. Maybe all you really need to know is that while having a Nerf gun war with students, I once shot a wasp out of the air in cold blood . . . with a Nerf gun. I also ate a can of wet cat food once, but I've mostly tried to block that experience out of my memory.

So, you can tell we aren't the fun police! In fact, these dudes are some of the most jovial men I've ever been around. We love to goof around and have fun, but we also write with a great burden and conviction that student ministry should be pursued with biblical categories in place.

The impulses that lie behind the creation of this book make for an ambitious endeavor. We are trying to kill two colossal birds with one stone: *Fulfill Your *Student Ministry* is meant to serve as both a manifesto and field guide. First, each chapter begins with a manifesto-like statement. Each statement is meant to clarify what student ministry should be in order to bring about maximal biblical health. Second, you'll perceive a rhythm in each chapter: (1) Raise a particular issue in student ministry, (2) provide biblical warrant for our position on that issue, and (3) wrap up with beginning steps for change—thus, a field guide.

CHAPTER 1

STUDENT MINISTRY, THE BIBLE, AND THE GOSPEL

Rechab Gray

Article I: A healthy student ministry values the gospel above all else and allows it to drive every element and aspect of the ministry rather than employing attractional forms of student ministry.

Student pastors believe the gospel. And yet, we often don't know how to infuse the reality of that good news into the workings of our ministries. In order to have holistically gospel-centered student ministries, we must be recognize how we fall short of this hope in our students' lives and in our own.

There are two primary pitfalls in ministry. We are either shooting for our ministries to be more reverent toward the Word or more relevant to the world. Neither is bad, but we must strive for both. If we are going to combat the current trend of students' simultaneous departures *for* college and *from* Christ, we must beware of the two ditches we often fall into.

Reverence-Based Student Ministry vs. Relevance-Based Student Ministry

I remember being in the deep south and going to see a play that at a local church. Each character had a short stint where their life was summarized, they died, and finally they were brought before God's judgment seat. I can only vaguely remember one character going to heaven, but I vividly remember multiple characters being tossed into hell.

One character was arrayed in 90's-style shades, a jean jacket, and MC Hammer-esque parachute pants. I loved everything about that guy because I was becoming more and more intrigued by everything hip-hop. In those days I even rocked my own flat top fade with a perfectly placed part. So, the guy they were sending to hell looked a lot like, well, me. The one person going to heaven did not look like me.

We are all familiar with churches like these. They mean well but have taken the fear of the Lord to an unhelpful place. And while these ministries are unfortunate—outliers, hopefully—our own ministries can have the same repulsive effect even if our methodology differs. We make sure our teaching is not "watered down." We emphatically draw the line between what culture teaches and what Christ teaches. And yet, could it be possible that as we have a reverence for the Word, we have lost our reference point to the gospel?

Well, it *is* possible. It is admirable to want the entirety of your ministry to be shaped by the Scriptures rather than societal fads. It is awesome that the Bible is the primary text used in teaching at your student gatherings. It is amazing that you have been able to "keep the main thing the main thing" in a church culture that is so adept at majoring on minors and minimizing the transcendent. However, it is possible to preach the Word that was inscribed and miss the Word that was incarnated. Why does it say, "The word is near you in your mouth and in your heart" (Rom 10:8)? Because it *is* possible to teach holiness and yet unload truckloads of grace too.

On the other hand, some ministries build their entire program on how to be relevant, fun, engaging, and—here goes that word—cool. In my city there is a ministry that reaches over 100 students each week. It is a beautiful thing to see. Kids from all different backgrounds are coming together in the same church building. When the church beats out the after-school programs, athletic activities, and the like, it must be doing something right, right?

The great commission isn't *only* about reaching. It's also about teaching. Discipleship is a two-way street. It involves both learning and instructing. It demands that the disciple adhere to the instruction of the disciple maker. Relevance-based ministries tend to expect little to nothing from their program attendees. Are such ministries really "reaching" students?

A ministry based on relevance risks making a biblically ineffective connection. It's great to reach the lost. It's great to go after the "unchurched." It's great to engage this generation in a way that speaks to them. But if it's all fun, all relevance, and no reverence, we are in danger of trading gospel-based ministry in for gimmick-based ministry.

Gospel-Based Student Ministry

The gospel says that man is so *lawless* that Jesus came to die for us (1 John 3:4–5). The gospel also says that man is so *loved* that Jesus came to die for us (1 John 3:16). Christ doesn't minimize lawlessness so that he can be more relevant. Neither does he minimize his love so that he can be more reverent. He was holy in that he understood sin's severity and relevant in that he took that sin upon himself. The gospel meets us right where we are. It says that evil is so serious that it cost Jesus everything, but his love is so ultimate that he gave us everything. It is both serious and suitable, both lawful and liberating. Ultimately, gospel-centered student ministry should be both Word-driven *and* world-driven: driven *by* the Word and driven to the world! Ministers must relay the relevant word in a reverent way. Esteeming one over the other misses the point!

The Ever-Reverent and Relevant Gospel of God

Now, in order to be both reverent and relevant, we must study society like we study the Scriptures.

But in studying society, we must not be content with merely "being real" with our audience and not calling them to righteousness. This would make the good news just reliable news—a nice, cool story with nothing actually good about it. So how do we make this gospel relevant to our students? I think Paul models this well in 1 Corinthians.

In this book Paul is addressing the Corinthian church. They are facing issues that would destroy any local church. If you think your student ministry is facing moral issues, be assured that your students' holiness looks like that of the heavenly seraphim in comparison to this church! Yet Paul writes to them saying, "I give thanks to my God always for you because of the grace of God that was given you in Christ Jesus" (1 Cor 1:4).

How is he able to give thanks? What is the nature and foundation of this "grace?" Chapter 15 provides the answer:

> Now I would remind you brothers of the gospel I preached to you, which you received, in which you stand, and by which you are being saved . . . If Christ has not been raised, then our preaching is in vain and your faith is in vain . . . But in fact

> Christ has been raised from the dead. (1 Cor 15:1–2a, 14, 20a)

Paul then goes on to talk about how we will be raised to life in a manner like Christ. He uses the analogy of planting a seed that grows into something far greater—a tree. He concludes his argument with these beautiful words:

> So it is with the resurrection of the dead. What is sown is perishable; what is raised is imperishable. It is sown in dishonor; it is raised in glory. It is sown in weakness; it is raised in power. It is sown a natural body; it is raised a spiritual body. (1 Cor 15:42–44)

He continues:

> I tell you this, brothers: flesh and blood cannot inherit the kingdom of God, nor does the perishable inherit the imperishable . . . When the perishable puts on the imperishable, and the mortal puts on immortality, then shall come to pass the saying that is written:

> "Death is swallowed up in victory."
> O death, where is your victory?
> O death, where is your sting?"
>
> The sting of death is sin, and the power of sin is the law. But thanks be to God, who gives us the victory through our Lord Jesus Christ.
>
> Therefore, my beloved brothers, be steadfast, immovable, always abounding in the work of the Lord, knowing that in the Lord your labor is not in vain. (1 Cor 15:50, 54–58)

See, Paul gives thanks for this church because he knows they are destined for the good news of resurrection life. He's able to look beyond their momentary sins because the glory to come is incomparable. Where someone is showing signs of perishing, dishonor, and weakness, Paul is able to respond to them with a reminder of the future imperishable, powerful, glorious resurrection found in Christ! This future picture of glory fuels present practice in the world. The salvific grace of God in Christ changes a person in the here and now!

He goes on to apply that same grace to every issue they are facing. Each time he brings up an issue, he points to how Jesus has already overcome that issue in his cross and resurrection work. We should implement his approach in our ministries: If there are divisions in the church, remember that Christ is the only foundation that our ministries should be built on (3:11). If a student is conceited, remember that they are Christ's and have nothing to boast in besides him (3:22). If they judge themselves greater than another, remember it is Christ who will ultimately judge the world and bring all things into the light (4:5). If sexual immorality is present (and believe me, it is), tell them that the Passover lamb has been slain and has called us to celebrate the festival with the unleavened bread of "sincerity and truth" (5:1–8). For those who want to live like the world, remind them that Christ has justified, sanctified, and washed them (6:11). I can go on and on. I won't. This is the model for ministry! Honor the work of Christ by applying that work to people's lives. Here are some practical ways to apply this to your ministry now.

Next Steps

Preach with gospel-centrality

So often we think we need to wait until the end of our message to call unbelievers to receive Jesus Christ. This type of sermon is helpful but not a fully gospel-centered message, for it says nothing about how the gospel applies to the believer. One way to make sure that both believer and unbeliever see how Christ impacts their lives is to preach Christ as *model*, *mediator*, and *means* in every message you deliver.

When you preach, make sure you are showing how Christ perfectly *models* your primary application point. If Christ hasn't modeled it, you might be prescribing too much. For example, if you are preaching on lying, mention that Christ is called the Truth. Scripture says that he never sinned, "neither was deceit found in his mouth" (Is. 53:9). Christ is our perfect example.

Then show how Christ is the *mediator* for us in the ways we have failed to follow His example. "Though he never lied, he died for liars like you and me. Every lie was placed on his limbs. Every utterance of deceit was paid for at his death."

Finally, show that he doesn't only give grace that exonerates but grace that empowers. "He rose from the dead, putting deceit to death and giving the Spirit of Truth, that you might not bear false witness but bear witness to the truth, bringing life to a dying world." He is the *means* by which we can live this out.

Change the Culture, Not the Program

Often, the first thing we look at when trying to change a ministry is the program, but what really needs to change is the culture of your student ministry. In order to do this, student pastors need to be the model. Having leaders go through books by gospel-centered authors is a great way to begin.

Along with this, periodically ask your students the hard questions. Ask them to explain the gospel in their own words. Ask them if they feel like the Word of God is taken seriously at the ministry they are a part of. Ask if the Word of God is being taught in a way that addresses their immediate concerns and issues. Ask what issues aren't being addressed from Scripture. I have found students will be honest in response to these types of questions.

Encourage "Gospel Freestyling"

When Eminem was younger, he would go on various radio stations around the country, and they would challenge him to rap on the spot. This is an art called "freestyling." To make it really challenging, they would show him an object, and he would have to begin rhyming words with that object in a way that connected back to his overall flow.

We should cultivate an environment where our volunteers are able to do the same in conversations, teachings, and small groups. We should work to take any given topic and bring up how the significance of Christ's life, death, and resurrection directly impacts that given issue. That is called gospel fluency, and we must get to a place where our staff and volunteers are fluent in this language!

Conclusion

Understanding which ditch—relevant or reverent—your church and student ministry tends to fall into is important. Be hard on yourself. If your students aren't inviting their friends ask, "Why not?" Are we failing to reach them where they are? Has the Word of God become musty to them? If Scripture is living and active, it should be proclaimed in a lively and active way. On the other hand, is your ministry busting at the seams, but no one is being transformed? Is discipleship your greatest weakness? It might be that your ministry has lost reverence for the Word of God. Holiness is not a priority. Either way, there is hope. God has not left you. God cares more about the students in your care than you ever could. Repent where necessary, make the appropriate changes in your own life, and let this overflow to your team.

CHAPTER 2

STUDENT MINISTRY, THE BIBLE, AND THE LOCAL CHURCH

H. Jared Bumpers

Article II: Healthy student ministries prioritize integrating students into the life of the church upon becoming covenant members because they carry the same responsibility and privileges as adult members. Baptism and church membership are not mere obligatory rites of passage but rather bring covenant responsibilities.

Introduction

Connor was in middle school and lived down the street. His single father was raising him, and neither he nor his dad had a clue about God, the gospel, or church. My wife and I reached out to them and started to build a relationship with them. We loved them, served them, and invited them to church. Eventually, Connor came to church with us. It was clearly one of the first times Connor had ever been in a church service. He seemed lost during the singing and distracted during the preaching. Then, it happened. Out of nowhere, I heard the crunch. I looked over, and Connor was munching down on a big red apple mid-sermon. I guess I failed to mention that mid-service snacks (especially loud, crunchy ones!) are not typical. The only thing that would have made the whole event better is if the sermon was on Genesis 3!

Connor may not have understood the significance of corporate worship or the necessity of the local church, but those who lead and serve in student ministry must not miss the supreme value of the church as it relates to developing students into fully devoted followers of Jesus Christ. Corporate worship, opportunities to serve the body, fellowship, church discipline, and a host of other facets of the church are essential to connect students to Christ. Any approach to student ministry that fails to recognize the value of corporate worship and the importance of the church in the spiritual formation of students is faulty and needs to be abandoned.

Unfortunately, many churches, student pastors, and youth workers have lost sight of the value of students attending corporate worship, serving the body, and engaging in fellowship. Students no longer worship with the body. Student worship services and student small groups replace corporate worship and church involvement. Student ministries essentially function in isolation from the rest of the church body. This has to change.

Churches and pastors must view students as an integral part of the body now, not as merely future contributors. If they are members of the church, they are not simply the future of the church; they are its present. They are just as capable of attending, serving, giving, and growing as the adult members in the church. Student ministries must commit to connecting student-aged believers to the church as a whole. But how? The answer is simple: integrate students into the body quickly after they believe the gospel, help students embrace the purpose and the mission of the church, and unleash students to serve the body and share the gospel.

Connect Believing Students to the Body Quickly

Churches should make sure students understand the gospel prior to baptism. Once the pastors and youth workers are confident the student believes the gospel and evidences repentance, that student should be baptized and admitted into church membership. Students who are members can enjoy all the privileges of membership, but it must be stated that church membership also comes with serious responsibilities. Students who are church members are under the care of their pastors. They are subject to church discipline. They cannot blame their sin or disobedience on youth or ignorance. If professing students are not willing to submit themselves to church leadership or subject themselves to church discipline, they should not be baptized and should not be allowed to join the church. Students who believe the gospel, are baptized, join the church, and submit to church leadership and discipline, however, should be connected to the body and accepted into membership.

In the New Testament, those who professed faith in Jesus Christ were baptized shortly thereafter. Those who heard the gospel preached on the Day of Pentecost and responded in faith were baptized immediately (Acts 2). The Ethiopian eunuch believed in Jesus Christ and was baptized immediately (Acts 8). Likewise, students who respond to the gospel in faith should be baptized as soon as possible. To delay their baptism is to question the legitimacy of their conversion and keep them from publicly identifying with Jesus Christ. Instead of keeping students at a distance, churches and student ministries should seek to incorporate students into the body sooner rather than later.

Answer the "Why" and "What" Questions

Student pastors should also help students embrace the purpose and mission of the church. Why does the church exist? What is the church's mission? Helping students answer these two questions, and then wholeheartedly embrace the answers, is crucial to developing a healthy student ministry. Let's consider each of those questions individually.

First, why does the church exist? It exists to glorify God, which is the same reason you and I exist. Every single part of creation exists to bring glory to its Creator. As Paul wrote in Romans 11:36, "For from him and through him and to him are all things. To him be the glory forever. Amen." This includes the church, which is why Paul also wrote, "To him be glory in the church and in Christ Jesus to all generations, forever and ever. Amen" (Eph 3:21).

Therefore, the church—as well as the individual members who comprise the church—exist to glorify God. This means students do not exist for themselves. Their lives are not meant to be self-centered but God-centered. As members of the body and followers of Jesus Christ, their purpose is to glorify God and enjoy him forever. Student ministries must help students grasp the glorious reality of God's love and purpose for the local church.

Second, what is the mission of the church? Put simply, the church's mission is to make disciples of all nations. Jesus commanded his disciples, "Go, therefore, and make disciples of all nations, baptizing them in the name of the Father and of the Son and of the Holy Spirit, teaching them to observe everything I have commanded you. And remember, I am with you always, to the end of the age" (Matt 28:19–20). This commission still stands as the marching orders for the church. It does not come with an expiration date. The church is called to make disciples, which means students within the church are called to make disciples. Student ministries must call young people to join the church in its mission of making disciples of all nations.

Students need to be drawn into a world where they are no longer at the center; God is. Students need to be pushed to embrace God's mission of making disciples from every tongue, tribe, and nation. Student ministries play a vital role in this process. The key is to clearly communicate these truths and challenge students not just to affirm them but to grab them and own them.

Unleash Students to Serve and Share

Finally, student ministries need to change the way they think about their role. They don't exist as a daycare for teenagers or religious entertainment for students; they exist as training centers for gospel soldiers. Student ministries should train students to make disciples, and then they should unleash them to serve the body and share the gospel with an unbelieving world.

Paul invested in Timothy, and then he unleashed him to do ministry. Yes, Timothy was young, but Paul told him, “Don’t let anyone despise your youth, but set an example for the believers in speech, in conduct, in love, in faith, and in purity” (1 Tim 4:12). Age wasn’t an issue. Timothy could still pastor a church and set an example for other believers, even though he was young (yes, Bible nerd, I know “youth” could be any age up to forty, but the point remains: age does not prevent someone from living a godly life and providing an example for other believers). Students are capable of serving in the church, sharing the gospel with unbelievers, and making disciples in the present.

Churches and student pastors, please stop treating your students like unbelievers. Stop holding them back from church service and ministry opportunities. Train them to make disciples, and then unleash them. Unleash them to serve the body. Unleash them to share the gospel. Unleash them to wreak havoc on the kingdom of darkness.

Next Steps

I've tried to address what I perceive to be a problem in many churches and in many student ministries: the isolation of students from the church. Students and student ministries seem to be disconnected from the rest of the body of Christ. In this last section, I want to provide four practical steps to address this problem. While additional steps could be added, these steps should help student ministries move towards a healthier, more connected relationship with the church as a whole.

Baptize Students and Accept Them into Membership . . . but Be Careful

I know I've already addressed this, but let me drive home the point: students should be baptized and received into church membership after a credible profession of faith. If a student can clearly articulate the gospel and evidences faith in Jesus Christ, churches should baptize that student. Celebrate his or her confession of Christ as Lord. Let's follow the New Testament by baptizing and accepting into membership those who confess Christ, regardless of their age . . . but be careful! Do not forget that baptism and church membership involve accountability and church discipline (Matt 18:15–20). Students must be held accountable, and even disciplined, when they remain in unrepentant sin.

Keep Students in Corporate Worship on the Lord's Day

One huge step to connecting students to the church is to encourage them to participate in corporate worship each week. "Youth services" that occur at the same time as corporate worship fails to value the unity and cross-generational nature of the local church. There are multiple problems with this approach. First, in this model students rarely hear their pastor(s) preach. Some churches also provide alternative services for children, which means kids rarely hear their pastor preach until they are out of high school. Second, students rarely worship with their family. They never get to watch their mom and dad sing songs of worship to God or see their parents listen attentively to the preaching of the Word in church. They rarely get to watch their mom and dad participate in the Lord's Supper or hear their parents pray during corporate prayer. Finally, in this church model students are kept from seeing the diversity of the body, particularly its intergenerational element. Keeping students isolated from the body robs them of opportunities to see singles, young married couples, middle-aged married couples, and senior adults participating in worship and faithfully serving God.

Allow Students to Serve in Various Ministries

Students are not simply the future of the church; they are part of the church now. One way to demonstrate this is by allowing them to serve in the various ministries of the church. While this might sound easy, it can be more difficult than you think. Adults who oversee ministries may be hesitant to let young people serve, and students might not immediately jump at the chance to serve. Nevertheless, it is incredibly beneficial to allow students to serve while they are teenagers. As a student pastor, I had students serving on the welcome team, the media team, in the music ministry, in the children's ministry, and in the evangelism ministry. Many of these students still serve in those ministries. Involving students in ministry at a young age connects them to the body, gives them experience in ministry, and increases the likelihood of their staying in and serving the church when they graduate.

Seek Consistency between Student Ministry and the Church

Student ministries should seek to integrate the purpose of the church and the mission of the church into the fabric of their services and small groups. Rather than focusing on "fun and games," the student ministry should focus on glorifying God by making disciples. Youth services should mirror adult services, which means they should consist of reading, praying, singing, and preaching God's Word. Small groups should mirror adult small groups, which means they should consist of prayer, Bible study, spiritual conversations, and fellowship. Everything student ministries do should reflect the church's purpose to glorify God and the church's mission to make disciples.

Conclusion

One of the most oft-cited statistics in student ministry is the number of students who leave the church after graduation. I've heard numerous "experts" say that roughly 80 percent of Christian students leave the church after graduating high school (although I've not seen the data used to draw such a conclusion). I've often wondered, though, "How many of those students were growing, baptized, and integrated members of the church to begin with?" Sure, they may have attended student worship services. They may have been in a small group with other students. They may have participated in youth events. But were they really connected to the body? Were they really part of the church? Could it be that, in spite of our best efforts to make students feel welcome by offering alternative worship services and connecting them with other students and hosting activities for them, we have disconnected them from the church and contributed to their exodus? Let's remedy this by connecting students to the body, helping them embrace the purpose and mission of the church, and unleashing them to serve the church, share the gospel, and make disciples.

CHAPTER 3

STUDENT MINISTRY, THE BIBLE, AND DISCIPLESHIP

Sam Bierig

Article III: Healthy student ministries seek to cultivate a culture focused on life-on-life and one-on-one spiritual formation through Bible reading and prayer over event-driven and activities-based programs.

Jordan had one of those stories that's tough to wrap your mind around. He lived with his dad in a house that had massive holes in the floor and no functioning heat. His mom was absent from the picture, and on most nights Jordan wound up sleeping on the couch of whatever friend he bummed a ride home from football practice with that day. This was Jordan's survival pattern throughout high school until finally one incredible family from our church took him in for keeps.

I first met Jordan as a ninth grader. He came with a friend to one of our midweek student ministry gatherings. Before the service, I typically played dodgeball or basketball with the students who showed up early (my shoulder is still crunchy from launching light-weight Gator skin dodgeballs at students' heads). So, I challenged Jordan to a game of hoops, despite the fact that he was known around town as a pretty beastly athlete. And if memory serves me correctly, I decimated him 15-1. #StreetCred, am I right?

After that first Wednesday night, Jordan kept coming back. The real turning point, though, came when I asked, "Hey man, would you be interested in reading through the book of Matthew together?" To my shock, he excitedly said, "Yeah . . . for sure!"

The first time we met up, we walked through the storyline of the Bible as it unfolds along the lines of Jesus's genealogy in Matthew 1. He was taken aback by the unity and connectedness of the Bible.

That was the start of our one-to-one discipleship relationship. No pyrotechnics. No smoke machines. No program. Just two dudes and a Bible. Two dudes and Matthew 1. It was normal, and it was amazing.

Jordan eventually turned from his sin and entrusted his whole life to Jesus. I baptized him into the membership of our church. Our church members absorbed him into the life of our church. He fell in love with God's Word. He devoured it, in fact. He loved our church, and he loved to worship the Lord. In short, he became a disciple of Jesus Christ.

Jordan and I continued to meet together throughout his time as a high schooler. Most times, we met up at Burger King. Disciple making doesn't require a lot of money or a killer meet up space, and it sure isn't flashy. It's about consistently bringing your "Timothy" under the authority of God's Scriptures and letting his Word seep into every crevice and recess of his life. When your discipleship is about souls and Scripture, you're on the right track.

I have used this exact pattern of one-to-one discipleship dozens of times. When you put the simple study of the Bible at the center of your discipleship, you can be confident you're hitting the bullseye. Going about discipleship in this way takes all the guess work out of the equation.

In the interest of full disclosure: discipleship isn't always as smooth as mine and Jordan's story. "Abysmal failure" would be a good phrase to characterize my efforts with another guy. We worked through Colossians and then stalled out in the latter half of Proverbs. I tried to be faithful, but neither I nor the Holy Spirit seemed to get any traction with this guy. I had to settle for faithfulness on this one. But isn't that kind of the point? You can seed and water the field, but only God can bring the fruit (1 Cor 3:7). Charles Bridges said it well, "The seed may lie under the clods till we lie there, and then spring up." Don't become discouraged and stop seeding, student pastor. Trust the Lord. He'll bring growth in his time. Whatever you do, don't switch to some new, gimmicky, topical way of doing things. When your ministry is over and you stand before Christ at judgment, you'll be glad you built your disciple-making on the solid foundation of the Scripture.

What follows are six foundational principles for making disciples out of the students who darken the doors of your student ministry. I have only two objectives in this chapter: (1) I want you first to decide to invest your disciple-making efforts on souls and Scripture; and (2) I want you to be equipped to do what is commonly called one-to-one Bible reading. Only two things in this temporal world will outlast Christ's final judgment: souls and Scripture (1 Pet

1:24; John 5:28–29). Consequently, the wise student pastor invests his whole life into those two realities. He channels everything—all of his time, words, passions, and money—toward those two realities. He banks it all on this intersection, this critical zone, where the eternal and temporal collide. Our discipleship efforts somehow reach forward into the future of the new heavens and the new earth by investing in students in the here and now. So, tether your disciple making (souls) to what I am calling one-to-one Bible reading (Scripture). Because souls and Scripture are eternal, one-to-one Bible reading should be your go-to discipleship method. This is the center of the bullseye! Before we get into the thick of it with these principles and my proposal, it is important to make a few clarifications:

Clarification (1): What I mean by the word *discipleship*, or *disciple making* is more or less meeting up "one-to-one" for the purpose of studying the Bible. I will, at times, deviate from that meaning, but I will signal if I do so.

Clarification (2): It is unwise, and borderline immoral (1 Thess 5:22), for a male student pastor to meet with a female student alone for any purpose. I don't think we can be too careful in this regard. If we can learn anything from high profile moral failures, it is that men are to disciple men and women are to disciple women. I would include in this clarification male and female youth workers. It is extremely unwise for male youth workers to provide car rides for female students, and likewise for female youth workers to provide car rides for male students. I am not advocating for a position that leaves women pastorless, but I do want us to be wise. This will be further detailed in the last section.

Six Principles for Disciple Making in Student Ministry

Let the Word Do the Work

Student pastors are one-trick ponies (John 8:31–32). If you can't traffic in the transference of the Scriptures, you're not worthy of your post. It's that simple. From beginning to end, disciple making is all about investing God's Word into the lives of students. That's what Jesus has in mind when he says, "*teaching* them to observe everything I have commanded you" (Matt 28:20 CSB). Jesus has in mind relational investment tethered to the

Scriptures and embedded in the local church—that is discipleship. Isaiah 55:10–11 says,

> *For just as rain and snow fall from heaven and do not return there without saturating the earth and making it germinate and sprout, and providing seed to sow and food to eat, so my word that comes from my mouth will not return to me empty, but it will accomplish what I please and will prosper in what I send it to do.*

In Isaiah 55 we see that the Bible is a powerplant unto itself. All you need to do is plug your students up to that power. When our heavenly Father sends his Bible out on mission, it never fails to accomplish his intended objective, be it judgement, encouragement, rebuke, creation, or salvation. It cannot fail. As a student pastor or youth worker, all you need to worry about is consistency and faithfulness in execution—one biblical book after the other. Focus your efforts on the plain reading of Scripture. Don't let your discipleship be just "bro-ing out with the bros." Rather, Read → Interpret → Apply → Repeat. Because he does his work with his Word, the task is simple, though difficult at times.

And, ultimately, the fruit is up to him. So, *let the Word do the work.*

Focus on your Local Church

Because you are finite and have limited bandwidth, focus your disciple-making efforts, like a laser, on the members of your local church. In Titus 2:2–6, Paul paints a straightforward picture of discipleship in the local church:

> *Older men are to be self-controlled, worthy of respect, sensible, and sound in faith, love, and endurance. In the same way, older women are to be reverent in behavior, not slanderers, not slaves to excessive drinking. They are to teach what is good, so that they may encourage the young women to love their husbands and to love their children, to be self-controlled, pure, workers at home, kind, and in submission to their husbands, so that God's word will not be slandered. In the same way, encourage the young men to be self-controlled.*

Disciple-making in the local church, then, is cross-generational, familial, intentionally gender conscious, and holiness driven. In Titus, discipleship takes place inside a local church with real and normal pastors (Titus 1:6–9), preaching (Titus 2:1), church discipline (3:10), and presumably the whole ecclesial nine yards.

It might be tempting to overlook that fact, but for many student pastors this is one of those truths hidden in plain sight. With all the stellar parachurch ministries out there, it might seem easier to hitch your disciple-making wagon to one of those, but I want to caution you against that tendency. God is saying through Paul that he wants to promote a vision where local church pastors' disciple-making energies are best channeled toward his local church. Parachurch ministries have their use in the kingdom, but Jesus didn't promise to come back for a parachurch ministry. He *did* promise to come back for his bride, the church—which looks like Titus 2. Keep your focus where Jesus's heart is—the local church. *Focus on your local church.*

Live a Compelling Life

Student pastor, if you look over your shoulder and do not see a pack of young Christian students trailing you—ones who are hungry for the glory of Christ and his Word—then it might be because you don't live a very compelling life. You have precious little to disciple students toward if you don't have a biblically saturated, compelling life.

This generation craves an all-encompassing, compelling vision for life. They are entertained nearly to death, and they know entertainment is but castles of sand in the end. They desire a vision and purpose they can throw their whole lives into. This is even more true in the church, of course (John 13:35). Christians know that life in Christ is the only soul-satisfying game in town (John 6:68–69). All visions and purposes outside of Christ (Col 3:4)—world peace, world hunger, human flourishing—buckle under the weight of the glory. Only Jesus is worthy of being a "living sacrifice" for.

Your marriage, mission, money, hobbies, and home, then, are stages in the grand theater of life, and your students are watching your playwriting. Accordingly, "cool" crumbles under the critical eye of your students, but a biblically compelling life bears up under the scrutiny. So, student pastor, wield your life in a way that is compelling to emulate (1 Pet 3:15). *Live a compelling life.*

Be Selective

In 2 Timothy 2:2 Paul tells Timothy to be selective in his discipleship efforts. He says, "What you have heard from me in the presence of many witnesses, commit to *faithful* men who will be able to teach others also." He doesn't say invest in every single church member, to the same degree, at all times, everywhere. No, he tells Timothy to entrust the ongoing ministry of the gospel to "faithful men." Why would Paul be so rude as to suggest Timothy be selective? Paul knows Timothy is tethered—as you are—to basic time and bandwidth constraints. Timothy isn't omnipresent, and you aren't either. He had to make tough calls, and so will you. It is not insensitive to be selective with your discipleship efforts. It is humble, wise, and discerning. Take this principle straight out of Paul's playbook and apply it. *Be selective.*

Bleed for This

Impacting student lives requires sacrificial and intentional inconvenience. Therefore, time and money are the necessary skin that student pastors must invest in the game of discipleship. The good news is, time and money happen to also be the most effective tools you've got in your disciple-making toolbelt.

Matthew 6:19–21 says,

> *Don't store up for yourselves treasures on earth . . . But store up for yourselves treasures in heaven, where neither moth nor rust destroy, and where thieves don't break in and steal. For where your treasure is, there your heart will be also.*

If you could view your life from eternity-future, you would see yourself being glad that you used your time and money for disciple-making (James 5:5).

- *Pick up the tab.* When you meet weekly with your "Timothy" to study, you should buy his coffee/meal. This will go a long way in how your disciple perceives your love and care for his soul.
- *Buy them a study Bible.* Further, buy any materials needed. I suggest you buy your disciple a good study Bible.
- *Provide a ride if needed.* Of course, as mentioned above, you must employ biblical wisdom by allowing gals to disciple gals and guys to disciple guys. With that clarification stated, providing

a ride to and from meetings might eliminate impediments to consistency.
- *Move them in with you.* My wife and I bought our home with this idea in mind. Thus far, four different church members have lived in our home. It goes a long way in the life-on-life way of discipling.

You're going to have to bleed for this just a bit.

Train up an Army

You don't have the capacity to disciple every student in your student ministry in the way I have proposed in this chapter. You're going to need to train up a whole army of disciplers. So, as the student pastor, you lead the way in creating the discipleship culture in your church's student ministry. If you lead, then your students and student workers will follow you as you follow Jesus. That means you must organize and enlist church members who live holy and compelling lives for the task of making disciples out of the students in your church. *Train up an Army.*

Next Steps

Start with Small Biblical Books

Start with Colossians, Jonah, or Ruth. This way you'll get a quick win under your belt. Starting with smaller books provides that sense of completion and hope that is needed for tackling bigger books. I suggest you start with Colossians. Ideally, you and your disciple would meet four weeks in a row. When finished, reevaluate and move onto John or one of the other smaller books.

Enlist Faithful Women

Equipping faithful older women to make disciples of the female students in your student ministry is a matter of pastoral fidelity for which you will give an account (Heb 13:17). These women must be doctrinally faithful, love the Bible, and live godly, compelling lives. They should push and prod the female students in your church toward growth in fellowship with Jesus. Start by calling a training meeting after church, provide lunch, and show these Titus 2 women how to go about one-to-one Bible reading.

Plan a Discipleship Group for Next Semester

You want to sow your students back into the membership and relational life of the church. But as you know, many of your student workers and church members do not feel equipped for this kind of discipleship. I suggest providing a meeting space where discipler and disciple can meet alongside others. You can lead the discussion in order to take the pressure off, but whatever you do, make sure to communicate clear expectations. This group option can be helpful in getting a culture of one-to-one discipleship kickstarted.

Find a Timothy and Get to Practicing

CHAPTER 4

STUDENT MINISTRY, THE BIBLE, AND PREACHING

Royland Kirkwood

Article IV: Healthy student ministries choose to preach expositional sermons and series through biblical books instead of emphasizing games, videos, and topical series.

On my bookshelf I have more than twenty books about student ministry. Some are helpful and thought provoking, offering advice and providing the purpose on how to sustain the student minister. However, out of those twenty books, only three mention the preaching of God's Word. At the very least, this shows that preaching is not a priority in student ministry.

I believe student pastors fall into one of two traps. First, we get caught up in a numbers game because we think the bigger the numbers, the more successful the ministry. Numbers are a factor of course, but they aren't the main thing. Second, we get caught up in entertaining students with our preaching rather than seeking their transformation (Rom 12:2). We all feel the pressure to be relevant when preaching to middle school and high school students, but that doesn't mean we have to preach sermons packed with jokes. When student pastors go for entertainment, the gospel is eclipsed. If our students remember our jokes and illustrations but can't remember the main point of the text, we have a problem. Fun and games are a part of student ministry; however, our primary goal is to lead students to be more like Jesus. Smoke machines, ProPresenter, a great student band, and amazing icebreaker games cannot penetrate the heart. Those tools have their place and can be helpful, but preaching God's Word should be the main course. Everything else is just appetizers.

I was eighteen when I first started preaching, and by nineteen I had taken my first full-time position as a student pastor. I'd only preached two sermons at that point, but I thought I knew it all. I was excited to be there, and the church was excited to have me. I learned real quick what mattered and what didn't. That first student gathering I had an amazing icebreaker and a great video lined up. But the ice breaker took twenty minutes, the video took fifteen minutes, discussion about the video took another twenty, and that left me with only five minutes to preach! That was the pattern for a typical service. I thought everything was going great until two students confronted me, "We're having a good time at Bible study, but are you going to teach us anything? We haven't learned anything new about the Bible since you've been here." At first I was offended, but I realized they were right. I was not trying to attract students to God's Word. I was trying to attract them to myself and to our events. This is where a lot of student pastors go wrong. We make fun and games primary. But everything should lead to the preaching of the Word, and everything should flow from the preaching of the Word.

Faithfulness: The Biblical Charge to Preach

To really understand the art of preaching, we need to start with what the Bible says about it. I want to focus on 2 Timothy 4:1–5:

> I solemnly charge you before God and Christ Jesus, who is going to judge the living and the dead, and because of his appearing and his kingdom: Preach the word; be ready in season and out of season; rebuke, correct, and encourage with great patience and teaching. For the time will come when people will not tolerate sound doctrine, but according to their own desires, will multiply teachers for themselves because they have an itch to hear what they want to hear. They will turn away from hearing the truth and will turn aside to myths. But as for you, exercise self-control in everything, endure hardship, do the work of an evangelist, fulfill your ministry.

Verse 2 doesn't say to preach what's trending. It says, "preach the Word." Pastors and student pastors tend to get caught up in preaching our own ideas rather than the actual Word. Paul, in his final words to his protégé, Timothy, gives him a serious, critical command, not a suggestion. Timothy must preach the Word because the Lord is watching. He also warns Timothy that he will have to stand before the Lord and answer for how he responded to this charge.

Paul wasn't talking just to Timothy. He was speaking to every man who has a call to preach. We don't have the option to preach anything but the Bible. We are commanded to preach one thing and one thing only—the Word. Philosophy, psychology, sociology, science, educational development, and current events are all important, but they are not going to save anyone. Our mission first and foremost is to preach the Word. We should be obsessed with preaching the Word. It should be the consuming passion of our life. H.B. Charles, Jr., said it well, "Our preaching is not the reason the Word works. The Word is the reason our preaching works." If there is one thing I don't want to hear when I stand before the Lord, it is that I was not faithful to preach his Word. Our preaching says a lot about who we are. Therefore, our seriousness or lack of seriousness toward biblical interpretation and proclamation matters.

There's a story told about a young violinist who came onto the stage and sat alone on a stool. He put his violin under his chin and played for an hour and a half. No music in front of him, no orchestra behind him, no breaks—just an hour and a half of absolutely beautiful violin music. After ten minutes or so, many critics put down their pads and listened like the rest of the audience. After the performance, the crowd rose to its feet and began applauding wildly—and they wouldn't stop. But the young violinist didn't acknowledge the applause. He just peered out into the audience as if he were looking for something—or someone. Finally, he found what he was looking for. Relief came over his face, and he began to acknowledge the cheers. After the concert, the critics met the young violinist backstage.

They said, "You were wonderful. But one question: Why did it take you so long to acknowledge the applause of the audience?"

The young violinist took a deep breath and answered, "You know I was really afraid of playing here. Yet this was something I knew I needed to do. Tonight, just before I came on stage, I received word that my master teacher was to be in the audience. Throughout the concert, I tried to look for him, but I could never find him. So, after I finished playing, I started to look more intently. I was so eager to find my teacher that I couldn't even hear the applause. I just had to know what he thought of my playing. That was all that mattered. Finally, I found him high in the balcony. He was standing and applauding, with a big smile on his face. After seeing him, I was finally able to relax. I said to myself, 'If the master is pleased with what I have done, then everything else is okay.'"[1]

It should be the same for us every time we prepare and stand to preach the Word. Is the Master pleased with us?

We are currently living out verses 3 and 4 of 2 Timothy 4:1–5, especially when it comes to students. They are turning away from the church and the message of Jesus Christ. People don't want to hear sound teaching, and there are false teachers aplenty. And Paul is absolutely right; people are turning away from sound teaching because they don't want to hear the truth. We are called not to preach what our audience wants to hear or what suits them, but rather the truth of the Word. We sometimes think our students can't handle the truth of the Word, but that couldn't be further from the truth. Notice that this text doesn't have an age limit. It doesn't say just preach to adults. Students need the gospel just like adults. Students sin just like adults. Every biblical text from Genesis to Revelation can be preached to a student, so don't hold anything back. Preach it all to them. Steve Lawson says, "The Bible is shallow enough for a new believer to wade in, but deep enough for a theologian to drown in."[2]

Finally, 2 Timothy 4:5 ends with three words we should always have in our minds: "fulfill your ministry." We are called to complete our ministry.

We are to carry out our ministry to the very end and fully perform all our duties. But know that you can never fulfill your ministry if you are not faithful in preaching the Word. When God judges our preaching, it's pass or fail. He will not give us letter grades. We will either be faithful or unfaithful.

Preach Expositional Sermons to Your Students

While planning for the launch of a new student worship service, my senior pastor and I were working on a potential preaching calendar. I submitted a draft to him that I thought had a good variety of texts and topics. He didn't like it. The texts I had chosen didn't match the topics I had chosen. Then he suggested that I start by preaching my way through the Sermon on the Mount. I thought that the Sermon on the Mount might not exactly pique our students' interest . . . might be too much for them to comprehend. How could a twelve-year-old or seventeen-year-old relate to the Beatitudes, the law, adultery, divorce, oaths, and fasting? Well, we eventually launched the student worship service, and turns out he was right. The response was amazing. This was the perfect text to preach to young people! Our goal should be to get the text right and recognize that application will follow. The most effective way to do that is expository preaching.

Expository preaching is simple: it means to draw out the clear, God-intended meaning of the text so hearers can know and obey God. In his book *Encountering God Through Expository Preaching*, Jim Orrick asks, "What is preaching?" He answers, "Preaching is when a holy man of God opens the word of God and says to the people of God come and experience God with me in this text."[3] We often go down rabbit trails in sermons trying to reach students with something that the text was never meant to intend. Expository preaching, then, forces the preacher to stay in the text. Exposition is hard work, but I'd rather do the hard work and be faithful to the text than take the easy way out and be unfaithful.

Students are taking advanced English and reading, and some are taking chemistry and calculus. If they can understand those subjects, they can understand your sermon. To say that expository preaching doesn't speak to students is to say that the Bible doesn't speak to students. Therefore, expound on what the Bible says. The effectiveness of our sermons comes down to how well we prepare. There should are no excuses for not being prepared. We have far more access to information and resources than those that came before us. Student pastor, preach the Word!

Next Steps

Plan a Preaching Series

Here are five sermon series that will not only help your students but will help you as well. I would also mention that you need to have a preaching calendar that lays out what you are preaching at least three months ahead. This will help you to focus because you don't have to hunt down what text to preach each week.

1. The Sermon on The Mount (Matthew 5–7, 9 Sermons)
2. Ruth (4 Sermons)
3. The Ten Commandments (Exodus 20:2–17)
4. Jonah (4 Sermons)
5. The Seven Churches in Revelation 2–3 (7 Sermons)

Example Preaching Calendar (The Beatitudes)

Sermon 1 | Blessed Are the Poor in Spirit | Matthew 5:3
Sermon 2 | Blessed Are Those Who Mourn | Matthew 5:4
Sermon 3 | Blessed Are the Meek | Matthew 5:5
Sermon 4 | Blessed Are Those Who Hunger | Matthew 5:6
Sermon 5 | Blessed Are the Merciful | Matthew 5:7
Sermon 6 | Blessed Are the Pure in Heart | Matthew 5:8
Sermon 7 | Blessed Are the Peacemakers | Matthew 5:9
Sermon 8 | Blessed Are Those Who Are Persecuted for Righteousness | Matthew 5:10
Sermon 9 | Blessed Are You | Matthew 5:11–12

Read Books on Expository Preaching

On Preaching by H.B. Charles Jr.
Encountering God Though Expository Preaching by Jim Scott Orrick, Brian Payne, and Ryan Fullerton
Power in The Pulpit by Jerry Vines
Student Ministry that Matters by Ben Trueblood

Gospel Centered Youth Ministry by Eric McKiddie and John Neilson

Listen to Podcasts on Preaching

The On Preaching Podcast with H.B. Charles Jr
Expositor with Steven J. Lawson
Preaching and Preachers by Jason K. Allen

CHAPTER 5

STUDENT MINISTRY, THE BIBLE, AND WORSHIP

David Bronson

Article V: Healthy student ministries value student worship services that reflect the Sunday morning worship service of the church over entertainment-based programming.

Several years ago, I was leading worship at a student event. There were about 100 students in the room singing their guts out, and my emotions were running hot. As we finished the song, the speaker was supposed to come up to deliver the message, so I launched into a prayer. It began something like this: "Lord, thank you for sending *cross* to die on the *Christ*."

Now, this wasn't a serious slip of the tongue—we've all had moments like this—but for some reason my brain went into vapor lock and I blurted out, "Well, dang it." Except I didn't say "dang."

(The Bible says don't judge, okay?!)

While this wasn't the worst thing that ever happened to me in student ministry, it was certainly a lesson: never try to cover up one mistake with another mistake!

I'm afraid the Western church has done something similar in how we've approached worship in student ministry. We've all read the statistics that show that students are less engaged with church than ever. And we've read all the critiques about "what's wrong" with church or all the ways that the church just isn't "relevant." So, out of a wonderful desire to bring students to Christ, we've pursued all kinds of methods and formulas to overcome the perceived failures of the church and get them the gospel. The irony is that, as we worry ourselves sick to find what "works," we've abandoned that gospel—the very power of God according Romans 1:18!—in favor of human strategy.

Don't get me wrong. I'm not saying that we've defaulted on the *content* of the gospel message. I mean that we've tried to draw students to our churches with something *other than* the gospel. We try to attract and keep students with cool events, expensive giveaways, slick audio-visual presentations, and worship ministries. But all of these things are focused on being relevant, engaging, and fresh instead of on edifying to our students, strengthening to our churches, and glorifying God.

This approach to worship—focused on music as a tool to attract and keep students instead of the biblical discipline that it is—is cancerous to the student and destructive to the church. But why? And how do we do it differently?

A caveat: "worship" is an incredibly broad word. For the purposes of this chapter, when I say "worship" I'm referring to the time believers spend together singing to the Lord.

The Rise of Student-Centered Worship

As you might already know, worship in an exclusively student-centered context is the new kid on the church's block. Student ministry in its modern, most recognizable form began in the 1940's with an organization called Young Life, which used things like student worship services and attractional methods to draw students to the church.[4] These worship services were intentionally *counter-cultural* to church norms at the time: where “traditional” churches were still banging away on that piano or pumping the organ under the leading of an older saint with a hymnal, Young Life used guitars, drums, and new worship choruses.

This way of doing student ministry swept the church in the twentieth century, and now student worship ministries are nearly ubiquitous. In a way, you and I are retreading the footprints of organizations like Young Life and, later, Willow Creek and the “seeker-sensitive” movement.

Never before in history have churches spent so much time, effort, and money on putting together worship services solely for students. We have student worship bands, student worship pastors, student worship nights. We tune these events to the aesthetic that we believe will appeal to students.

But have we critically examined whether or not the Word backs up this approach? As a matter of fact, when you ask your students what worship is about—that is, *why* we're making all this fuss and bother—do they really know what we're even trying to accomplish? Let alone what God's Word says about it?

I would suggest that—even if we would never say this, even if we're not consciously aware of it—the way many churches approach worship in student-ministry settings actually communicates that worship exists *for their satisfaction* instead of the glory of God and the spiritual growth of his church.

Even if we say with our mouths that worship serves a greater purpose than our gratification, our budgets disagree. And we've told them as much. Almost everything we do communicates it.

The Corporate Worship of the Church

In contrast to the current student-centered approach to worship, the church has, for most of its history, focused its resources instead on *corporate* worship.

When I say "corporate," I don't mean "corporate" as in a business. Instead, I use the word in line with its Latin root *corpus*, which means "body." The corporate worship of the church is its worship as a whole unit: young, old, married, single, male, female, all of us. The whole congregation gets together in one room and reads Scripture together, sings together, and sits under the preached Word of God together. This is the biblical pattern: you'll never find a New Testament example of one demographic in the local church separating itself from the body for its own worship time.

I tell you this because we need to understand that a student worship service or a student worship band *is not a must-have, biblically speaking.* By contrast, corporate worship *is* a biblically necessary. The New Testament can't conceive of a believer who's not participating in the worship of a local church!

Of course, a student worship service or a student worship band isn't a *bad* thing (unless it replaces your church's Sunday morning worship service—more on that later). But God's not scowling at you if you don't have a student worship band!

The Pitfalls of Student Worship Ministry

With that background, I believe student worship ministries sometimes *undermine* the corporate worship of the church—and the participation of our students in the body—instead of serving it.

What do we communicate when we set up separate worship services for students, whether on Sunday mornings or Wednesday nights? We tell them, though certainly not intending to, that *they are not full-fledged members of the body.* By segregating them into separate worship environments, we tell them that either "real" church is too lame for them to even want to be a part of it or that they're not a part of the "real" church yet. No wonder they leave once they age out of our student ministries!

Worse still, what do we communicate to our students when all of our effort and energy is spent on worship services that essentially amount to sanctified entertainment? We tell them, however inadvertently, that God and his church exist *for their satisfaction.*

Now, as I said before, I choose that phrase carefully. I do not mean to communicate that worship, for the Christian, shouldn't regularly be a joyful, uplifting, exciting experience as we reflect on the good news of what Jesus has done for us and all the implications thereof! But what happens when "all the feels" fade? What happens when they graduate from our high-octane student worship environment and find that worship in a cross-generational environment just isn't as immediately engaging? Or what happens when they just get burned out on the student worship "experience" and find that YouTube and Twitch have content that's way more entertaining?

This is, as far as God's Word is concerned, simply unacceptable.

A Biblical Look at Worship

In Ephesians 5:18b–20, Paul tells us, "[B]e filled by the Spirit: speaking to one another in psalms, hymns, and spiritual songs, singing and making music with your heart to the Lord, giving thanks always for everything to God the Father in the name of our Lord Jesus Christ." To trace his thought here, our worship is a result of having been filled with the Holy Spirit. And worship has two goals: (1) to build up one another ("speaking to one another") and (2) to glorify God for what He has done for us in the gospel ("giving thanks . . . to God the Father in the name of our Lord Jesus Christ").

When a church's corporate worship accomplishes these two goals, there are a few results. First, the church is strengthened in unity (this is the broader point of Paul's teaching in this section of Ephesians 5, after all). Second, its members grow in grace, love for one another, and gratitude to God. Third, and most important, Jesus Christ is brought the glory that he deserves!

Instead of spending so much time and effort on crafting exciting, emotional worship services, we ought to teach students about the beauty of the gathered church, the importance of her corporate worship, and give them opportunities to serve the whole church with their gifts and abilities. Our student worship services should, rather than trying to upstage our Sunday morning corporate worship, serve as classrooms or study halls for our students to learn how to more fully participate in the worship of the body!

Imagine your student ministry filled with students who had learned to love the body of Christ by worshiping *with* the body of Christ! Imagine students who were committed to the church and understood that the worship of the church was primarily about serving others in light of the gospel instead of about their own satisfaction. How different would the spiritual health of your student ministry be?

Next Steps

With that in mind, let me suggest four steps you can take to bring your student worship ministry more in line with the corporate worship of the church, and therefore, the command of Scripture.

Teach about Corporate Worship

If you want your students to be happy, holy, healthy members of the body of Christ, they're going to need to know how to participate fully in Sunday morning corporate worship. They're going to need a stout, well-rounded view of what gospel-centered worship is all about. And, by God's grace, you are in a position to teach them these things.

Teaching them is going to mean modeling the right behavior. So, formulate your student worship services to be similar to your Sunday morning worship gatherings—and if you have a special Sunday morning worship service for students only, I would implore you to end that service at once. Your students desperately need to worship with the body!

If you need resources, check out Mike Cosper's *Rhythms of Grace*. If you like your reading a little more dense, Bryan Chapell's *Christ-Centered Worship* is not only a thorough examination of corporate worship, it's also a great resource to help you construct your own student worship services.

Simplify

I am a huge believer in musical quality in our worship services where I pastor. Some variation of the sentence, "The gospel should be the only stumbling block!" comes out of my mouth with great regularity (to the chagrin of my longsuffering A/V team!). But high-quality music does not equal high production values.

In light of the premium that Scripture puts on the unity of the body in its worship, I think it's important to signal to our students that our student worship service is the optional item. One big way we can do this is by sticking to a small team of musicians and singers, or even by just using one worship leader with a guitar or piano. Depending on your context, this might also entail cutting back on some of the visual elements: DMX lighting, fog machines, dimmed house lights, and the like. Show your students what's most important—their voices singing together to worship God—by de-emphasizing what *isn't*.

Bring in Other Pastoral Staff

If your church has a worship pastor, he's your ally in this task. If he's willing, I'd suggest asking if he would lead worship semi-regularly for your student group. See if he'd be willing to help develop musically gifted students in your group. This is another way to signal that the student ministry is just a part of the larger church, and also allows your students to develop relationships with the other pastors responsible for the care of their soul.

And don't neglect to involve the senior pastor, either. While this is not directly related to worship per se, seeing the senior pastor delivering a message or two on a Wednesday or Sunday night will go a long way to reminding your students that they're participants in a greater whole. This in conjunction with point one will necessarily influence the way they think about corporate worship.

Unify Your Worship Repertoire—and Stick to the Gospel.

Finally, spend time carefully considering *what* you will sing. You could do all of the above things and still wind up with students who think worship is about them, simply because all the songs they sing say that it is! A good way to avoid this is by using the same songs your church uses on Sunday mornings. It's tempting to bust out that one Ascend the Hill song with the awesome guitar part, but if your worship pastor isn't using it on Sunday morning, there's probably a reason. (And it probably has to do with the fact that it's really hard for Joe Pewsitter to sing.)

If your church's Sunday morning worship repertoire is lacking in theologically robust, singable, God-glorifying songs, then just stick to songs that tell some aspect of the story of the gospel or unpack the implications of the gospel. If you need suggestions, look up my church's blog at lbcblog.org. Every week we post our order of service. You're welcome to lift any of the songs we use!

Conclusion

I hope this chapter encourages you with some measure of freedom. Know that while you have an obligation to teach your students about the worship of the church, you are *not* obligated to wrack your brain to manufacture an even cooler service than last week. Teaching is already a heavy burden without the insistent demands of an unhealthy outlook on student worship. Trade this in for the simplicity and beauty of a student worship ministry that serves the church as a whole!

CHAPTER 6

STUDENT MINISTRY, THE BIBLE, AND SEXUAL HOLINESS

Samuel Bierig

Article VI: A healthy student ministry emphasizes a culture of repentance and sexual holiness rather than a legalistic or guilt-driven purity culture.

Sex: The Cathedral of our Culture

I believe that almost every so-called "couple" in your student ministry should break up. In fact, I am in part judging the success of this chapter on whether or not your student ministry experiences a mass revival of good, old-fashioned breakups. Too harsh? Maybe. But before you cart me off to that loony bin in your head where you put crazy people, let's allow Jesus to speak to the issue.

Jesus says,

> *"You have heard that it was said, do not commit adultery. But I tell you, everyone who looks at a woman lustfully has already committed adultery with her in his heart. If your right eye causes you to sin, gouge it out and throw it away. For it is better that you lose one of the parts of your body than for your whole body to be thrown into hell. And if your right hand causes you to sin, cut it off and throw it away. For it is better that you lose one of the parts of your body than for your whole body to go into hell."*

If Jesus means what he says in Matthew 5:27–30, and I sense he does, then what most of your students call "dating" is more like a minefield lined with explosives than a "relationship."

Our world says to embrace and welcome every sexual impulse, but Jesus says that is spiritual shackles. Your students traffic all day long in a world that whispers all manner of false gospels in their ears. But none of these false gospels are as devastating and damning as the one preached by the false god of sex (1 Cor 6:18). These students who weekly stroll into your youth room are hourly summoned to worship this sex god in our culture's unhallowed cathedrals. But you and I know they will find no remedy there. It is a worship that will not satisfy. The god of sex has promised "the good life" to your students but has failed to deliver. It's a broken system, and it has fallen to you to deal with the fallout.

Hookups, Hang-ups, and Holiness

The most recent solution the church has generated in response to the culture's spiraling sexual chaos has been termed purity culture.[5] I recognize that so-called purity culture in the church today has taken something of a public beat down of late. And much of that push back is right and good, but not all of it. Repenting of teachings that have flung the church far afield from right doctrine and mission is critical to the health of the Church. If we were to name all the lamentable demonstrations of purity culture it would take up most of the pages in this book! Nonetheless, it is appropriate to catalogue a few just to be clear on what we're talking about—and to help us discern what to discard and what to salvage.

Purity culture, as a movement, brought, albeit probably well intentioned, a tendency toward self-righteous Pharisaism. This manifested in a "true love waits" mentality that often fostered false hope and/or false guilt, a ritualized emphasis on purity rings, various forms of sinful patricentricity (you'll want to look that word up; it's a toughie, but I couldn't find another word!), and everyone's favorite—the strange quest to restore the idiosyncrasies of colonial courting practices. These attempts at sexual holiness have often misfired because they lack (1) biblical texts and (2) categories for gospel forgiveness and repentance. They have often failed to protect the right things and at times allowed the wrong things to flourish.

My Story

The first time my wife and I kissed was in front of about 300 people. No, we weren't at a gameshow, I didn't find her at a nunnery, and we were not on a kiss cam at a baseball game. It was our wedding day.

Mal and I were, however, regrettably, not each other's first kiss. That is an important piece to our story.

Regarding purity culture, Mallory and I both read *I Kissed Dating Goodbye* and *Boy Meets Girl: Say Hello to Courtship* by Joshua Harris—before we met, actually. And although Harris has now tragically renounced Christianity, through common grace he got a few things right. The gospel was tellingly and stunningly absent, but he accurately diagnosed America's disastrous dating scene. Read in tandem, God used these books in my life. Despite Harris's failures, the book was at least a call to sexual purity. Mal and I needed to hear that at the time. Honestly, we have a perceptibly healthier marriage because of his influence. We endeavored to glorify Jesus in that purgatory-esque state of dating and waiting.

To say I don't regret waiting to kiss Mallory until our wedding day would be the understatement of the century! The way the Lord led us to pursue holiness in our relationship saved us from what might have been a thousand slow deaths of regret. However, we did not start out operating that way. If you back up in our story, you won't necessarily find faithfulness, wisdom, and sexual holiness. What you'll find is a lot of failure and repentance from sinful and foolish patterns. We felt a need for biblical wisdom in pursuing marriage and setting up wise boundaries for the waiting period. Our story is one of God's grace. He showed up in the lives of two broken believers, as he so often does, right when they needed him. He didn't wait for the two of us to be who we were supposed to be. He met us where we were.

What This Chapter Isn't Doing

What I don't wish to convey is that if you, one of your students, or anyone you know did not wait until marriage to kiss or have sex or sadly, they were sexually abused, that they are now somehow tarnished, broken, irrecoverable, or irreversibly soiled. Far from it! Jesus saves, and he saves to the uttermost. Period. No qualifications, no disclaimers, no take backs, and no caveats (Luke 7:36–50).

The gospel of Jesus Christ is an unsinkable hope for the sexually broken. And I am here to declare *that* hope will hold in the midst of every storm of sexual sin and brokenness. I know as a student pastor you are dealing weekly with all forms of sexual sin: pornography addiction, promiscuity, sexual abuse, same-sex attraction, gender dysphoria, and the list goes on. These difficult subjects are the reason we must know the mind of God on the matter.

We must maintain a high view of Jesus's mercy and justice *and* at the same time uphold his biblical commands on sexual holiness. They are not at odds. The importance of the Bible's teachings and implications for sexual holiness in our tumultuous culture cannot be overstated. To deny the Bible's call to sexual holiness is to deny Jesus's call to follow him and to therefore to deny Jesus himself (Matt 5:27–30).

Still, many of your students stumble into your church hopeless, hurt, and carrying more baggage than Southwest Airlines. Of all people, you, as a student pastor, ought to know how deep into darkness sin can take a soul. Don't pile on guilt and shame; they'll have enough of that on their own. Simply offer them a secure place to be a sinner saved by Jesus's grace. Remind them the church is not for perfect people but for repenters. Don't be surprised by their previous sexual forays and still-present tendencies. Listen to them, care for them, offer counsel, and be painstakingly patient, for if Jesus has already or soon grants them repentance, they are the new citizens of your Father's kingdom.[6]

You, as a student pastor, are tasked with the work of informing your students that they are not sexually ruined. Forever declare to them that "now is the day of salvation" and liberation from sexual sin and brokenness (2 Cor 6:2).[7]

Sexual Purity or Sexual Holiness?

Let's modify our lingo a bit. I propose we move away from sexual purity terminology to that of sexual holiness. Most of your students feel as though they've already blown it sexually—churched and unchurched alike. They think purity is not obtainable anymore. And though it is a subtle shift, thinking in terms of sexual holiness brings the reality of the Bible's teaching on the matter within the grasp of every repenter, and therefore holds out hope and gains a hearing more easily.

Moreover, sexual holiness is on offer to any student (John 4:1–26; 7:36–50), no matter what their past, if they repent of their sins, are indwelt by the Spirit of God, and live in accord with the fruit of the Spirit (Gal 5:13–25). This is why someone who leads a quite sexually reckless life before Jesus, upon conversion, can enjoy a remarkably fruitful and fulfilling sex life in marriage. On the other hand, it also explains why simply holding onto physical virginity until marriage does not automatically translate into a fulfilling sex life.

If handled lovingly and tactfully, the shift toward language of sexual holiness should lessen many of the impediments the purity culture movement unwittingly set up. It should move the conversation away from the over-torqued prominence of unsullied sexual virginity and toward a celebration of *strong families* and *churches* who value sexual holiness.

Let me offer a brief clarification of what I mean by sexual holiness:

> God's will for sexual holiness entails a wholistic commitment to biblically prescribed patterns of sexuality (i.e. chastity outside of marriage and heterosexual monogamy within marriage) to allow for maximal flourishing of every person, regardless of past sexual sin or failure.

If you notice, this vision seeks to bring about the highest degree of Christ-wrought joy for every person, particularly as they find themselves unmarried at this juncture. That is, I intentionally take the focus off sexual restriction and place it on sexual flourishing. At times, purity culture has involuntarily become more concerned with how, when, and where to set up restrictive fences than protecting something precious—one's holiness before a holy Lord. Moreover, this vision of sexual holiness seeks to emphasize repentance, not pristine purity.

A Biblical Vision for Sexual Holiness in a World Gone Mad

The most important passage in the Bible for your student's sexual holiness is found in 1 Thessalonians 4:3–7:

> For this is the will of God, your sanctification: that you abstain from sexual immorality; that each one of you know how to control his own body in holiness and honor, not in the passion of lust like the Gentiles who do not know God; that no one transgress and wrong his brother in this matter, because the Lord is an avenger in all these things, as we told you beforehand and solemnly warned you. For God has not called us for impurity, but in holiness.

Sexual unholiness starts in the heart and works outward in pursuit of our outer extremities. In 1 Thessalonians 4 the Holy Spirit is calling into question our treasured cultural practice of premarital kissing, time alone, and immodest clothing (for both female and male). For instance, the culturally accepted norm of kissing before marriage is a real dumpster fire of an idea. Kissing is the main way two lovers initiate the sequence of intimacy. God has wired us this way. So, giving an unwed couple license to kiss outside the safe confines of covenant marriage is like telling them, "Get inside your car, smash the gas pedal till the RPMs red line, but never, ever, ever put it in drive! Just turn the engine off immediately." That's ludicrous! Moreover, you'll never convince me that the male species can engage in kissing and maintain holy and God-honoring thoughts as they're simultaneously bombarded with sexual thoughts. Jesus says in Matthew 5:28 that anyone who "looks . . . lustfully" at another has already committed adultery. What Jesus leaves his hearer with in Matthew 5:29–30 is that his disciples must be ready to cut themselves off from anything that would keep them from sexual holiness.

The Holy Spirit raises the bar on sexual holiness in 1 Thessalonians. We are told, in no uncertain terms, that sexual holiness is *the will of God* for your students. So, if you have a so-called couple in your student ministry who consistently act out in sexually immorality, then you can without any hesitation tell them that it is God's will that they break up (I am speaking of junior and high school students. A couple in their twenties embarking on engagement needs to be handled with a little more nuance). So many people pray to know God's will, and here it is in this passage. It is that they pursue sexual holiness that reflects their salvation in Christ. What is the motivation for this? That you not wrong your brother or sister (church member!) "in this matter." God's justice demands it. What you are ultimately holding out to your student is the all-important truth that, Jesus is more. Jesus is more and better than gratifying their sexual impulses or fleeting desires.

Here are a few implications student pastors can derive from 1 Thessalonians 4:3–7:

1. First Thessalonians 4 puts to rest, forever, the question of "How far is too far?" It is the wrong question. The question your students should be

asking is, "What is holiness as the Lord sees it in Scripture?"

2. First Thessalonians 4 places a premium on the wisdom and necessity of setting up clear, communicated, and defined boundaries. Any "couple" who consistently breaks communicated and agreed-upon boundaries is in real spiritual peril. They are evidencing a lack of self-control (Gal 5:23). This also means boundaries aren't necessarily legalistic, they protect something of value—in this case, sexual holiness.
3. 1 Thessalonians 4 shows how reckless it is to cause someone else to stumble into sin. In Mark 9:42, we are told, "*Whoever causes one of these little ones who believe in me to sin, it would be better for him if a great millstone were hung around his neck and he were thrown into the sea.*" I don't know about you, but I want to help students avoid that.

Next Steps

Preach on Sexual Holiness and Dating

The Word of God changes hearts. I suggest you start by addressing sexual holiness and dating in your student ministry by preaching an expositional sermon series ("Waiting and Waiting"). Consider preaching through:

Proverbs 5–9
2 Samuel 11–15
Psalm 51

Make sure to press into the forgiveness found only in Christ, but do not fall to the temptation of blunting God's expectations for sexual holiness as found in these passages. We do ourselves and our students no favors by withholding the mind of God on these matters.

Memorize Passages pertaining to Sexual Holiness and Dating

When you preach the series I suggest above, consider passing out memory verse cards that pertain to sexual holiness and dating. Challenge your students to memorize and meditate on these passages.

Matthew 5:27–30

1 Corinthians 10:13

1 Thessalonians 4:3-8

Discuss Sexual Holiness and Dating

Proverbs 24:27 says, "Prepare your work outside; get everything ready for yourself in the field, and after that build your house." If a student can't sign a lease on an apartment or buy a house, are they really ready to take on the stewardship and care of a whole soul? You might be the only person in their life pushing them to think about biblical wisdom regarding sexual holiness.

Here are a few diagnostic questions to guide discussion with your students:

1. Is starting this relationship what's best for each other's holiness?
2. Are my actions propelling him or her to love God more?
3. Does the way I dress encourage others in pursuit of a holy thought life?
4. Will kissing each other be what's best in the long run? *Remind them they have no biblical right to kiss someone else's spouse.*
5. Is this relationship completely centered on God and his glory?
6. Are you growing in friendship, communication, and fellowship with other church members?
7. Are you clear on biblical roles as a husband and wife?
8. Are other people supportive of this relationship? *Godly church members, parents, other family members.*
9. Is there any presence of sexual unholiness in this relationship?
10. Do either of you have a pattern of pornography use?
11. What kind of accountability do you have set up?

Encourage your student(s) to focus more on being someone *worth* marrying and less on *finding* someone they think God ought to bring to them. If a teenage couple cannot answer "yes" to most of these questions, they probably are not in a healthy enough spiritual state to pursue a relationship.

Conclusion

The bottom line is this: As a student pastor, you must challenge the cultural norms of dating that lie dormant in your students and in many of their parents. Most of the ways that dating is carried out in our world is out of step with our Lord's call for sexual holiness. We are poor leaders of God's people if we do not address that fact. It is a delicate dance that requires wisdom, patience, tact, and, most of all, love to address matters of sexual brokenness and sexual holiness.

CHAPTER 7

STUDENT MINISTRY, THE BIBLE, AND MISSION TRIP

H. Jared Bumpers

Article VII: A healthy student ministry values local and global mission trips that focus on intentionally sharing the gospel over mission trips that primarily emphasize construction and service projects.

Introduction

My dad always said it was wise to learn from the mistakes of others. I still think this is a helpful piece of advice. Unfortunately, I haven't always followed that advice—especially as it relates to student ministry and missions. I hope I can save you some frustration and failure by sharing a blunder from early in my ministry.

During my first summer as a full-time student pastor, I decided to take my students on a mission trip. I am convinced of the truthfulness of Scripture and the power of the gospel (Rom 1:16), I know that Jesus changes lives (2 Cor 5:17), and I believe Jesus's command to go and make disciples still applies to followers of Jesus, including students (Matt 28:18-20). So, I was excited to take my students to engage in evangelism. I did a little research and found a mission organization that offered cheap trips to rural Kentucky. We loaded up the bus and headed to the Appalachian Mountains.

Looking back, the week really wasn't that bad. The lodging wasn't ideal. The food wasn't great. The camp speaker preached really long sermons from Ephesians 6 while wearing plastic Roman soldier armor (which was lame, although the real sword he used on the last day was legit!). Overall, the experience was good. The mission projects were well organized, and the sites were nice. There was just one problem: we weren't sharing the gospel! The projects were not evangelistic—they focused on acts of service. Our students were stretched and challenged to love others and serve people in need, but evangelism was virtually absent.

This encounter with student missions opened my eyes to the reality that not every trip that claims to be a mission trip is actually a mission trip the way the Bible conceives of one. Many organizations that claim to engage in missions are just facilitating long-distance service projects. After this experience, I was convicted that any future trips needed to focus on sharing the gospel with unbelievers. I remain convinced that churches should take their students on short-term mission trips that provide gospel opportunities, not just to serve others with acts of kindness or service projects.

Linking the Gospel and Missions

Student ministries need to avoid gravitating to service projects and make sure mission trips engage in mission work by sharing the gospel. This should be done by linking the gospel to service projects and refusing to separate the two. First, student ministries must be clear about the message of the gospel. In 1 Corinthians 15:1–3 Paul reminded the Corinthians of the gospel he preached to them:

> Now I want to make clear for you, brothers and sisters, the gospel I preached to you, which you received, on which you have taken your stand and by which you are being saved, if you hold to the message I preached to you—unless you believed in vain. For I passed on to you as most important what I also received: that Christ died for our sins according to the Scriptures, that he was buried, that he was raised on the third day according to the Scriptures, and that he appeared to Cephas, then to the Twelve.

Christ died for our sins, was buried, and rose on the third day. Student pastors and youth leaders must believe this message, teach this message, preach this message, and empower students to share this message.

Not only must student ministries be clear about the message of the gospel, they must be clear about the nature of the mission. Missions involves sharing the gospel, or it is not missions. In Acts 1:8 Jesus told his disciples they would "receive power when the Holy Spirit has come on you, and you will be my witnesses in Jerusalem, in all Judea and Samaria, and to the end of the earth." Jesus expected them to be gospel-centered missionaries. The book of Acts shows that Jesus's disciples committed themselves to be witnesses for Jesus and testify about what he did. One thing is clear in Acts: the gospel and evangelism are bound up in missions. They are inseparable. To participate in missions is to share the gospel, and a failure to share the gospel is a failure to do missions. This means that short-term student mission trips must include evangelism.

Three Dangers of Non-Evangelistic "Mission Trips"

It is inconsistent to preach about the power of the gospel and the need for missions, then turn around and take a mission trip that does not involve sharing the gospel. It's also dangerous.

First, mission trips that involve service projects rather than evangelism distort the gospel. They focus on what we do rather than on what Christ has done. Students are left thinking missions involves doing nice things and helping others, when in reality missions involves telling others about what Christ has done for sinners. Good mission trips make sure Jesus is the hero, not the ones serving him.

Second, mission trips that primarily consist of service projects rather than evangelism result in a focus on lesser needs (Mark 2:1–12). Let me be clear: I believe service projects and acts of mercy are the natural result of a transformed life. When substituted for evangelism on mission trips, however, these acts of service derail the purpose and heart of missions. They cause groups to focus on temporary physical needs rather than eternal spiritual needs. True mission trips focus on the gospel and making sure unbelievers hear the life-changing, eternity-determining good news of Jesus Christ.

Finally, student mission trips that focus on service projects distract students from evangelism and take work or ministry away from others. Students are given work assignments rather than opportunities to build relationships and share the gospel. Local churches are robbed of opportunities to love and serve their communities. Skilled workers (particularly in international contexts) are robbed of work and possible income. Everyone loses. All of these issues are avoided, however, if youth groups will take mission trips where sharing the gospel is the focus.

Next Steps

The power of the gospel and the command to share the gospel have not changed. Every Christian is called to go and share the gospel. We need student ministries that are committed to the gospel and captivated by a desire to train and unleash students to take the message of the gospel to the ends of the earth. These four practical steps will help students engage in missions.

Train Students to Love and Share the Gospel

Train your students to love and share the gospel. We cannot expect students to embrace evangelism and missions without training them to do so. This training should take place informally and formally. Informally, train your students to value Christ and the gospel through preaching and teaching opportunities. Your sermons and small groups should help students see the beauty of Christ, the power of the gospel, and give students a better appreciation of how Jesus transforms lives. Everything should be rooted in Scripture and centered on the gospel.

Train students to share the gospel in more formal ways as well. There are numerous evangelism models. You could teach them the "Romans Road," or they could follow the gospel outline used by J. I. Packer and Greg Gilbert.[8] Regardless of the model, it is helpful to give students a method for sharing the gospel. Do not just assume your students know how to articulate the gospel. Train them and give them tools to tell others about the person and work of Jesus.

Take Students away from Home to Share the Gospel

Student ministries shouldn't just train students to share the gospel; they should provide opportunities to do so! Youth leaders should plan local outreaches, and national and international mission trips so students can go and share the gospel. It isn't enough to affirm the importance of or preach on missions. Youth ministries must take students out of their comfort zone and away from their home to share the gospel and engage in missions.

I also think it is helpful to increase the depth of mission work as students progress through their student ministry. For example, a student ministry could have middle school students spend a week doing evangelism and ministry locally, high school students spend a week doing evangelism and ministry nationally, and college sharing the gospel and doing ministry internationally. At each level students are challenged to share the gospel and gain confidence to continue engaging in mission work at each new level.

Partner with Gospel-Centered Organizations

Find organizations committed to a gospel-centered approach to missions. As I mentioned in the introduction, not every organization that self-designates as a "mission organization" is actually a mission organization. Many of them are "service project" organizations. Churches that partner with these organizations are given opportunities to love and serve people, often in uncommon locations, but the students are not given opportunities to share the gospel. Make sure the organization that you partner with is actually a mission organization and will provide you with opportunities to build relationships and share the gospel.

Challenge Students to Consider Becoming Missionaries

During his earthly ministry Jesus emphasized the lostness of humanity and the need for laborers to share the gospel. He said, "The harvest is abundant, but the workers are few. Therefore, pray to the Lord of the harvest to send out workers into his harvest" (Matt 9:37–38). Students need to be presented with these two truths: (1) people are lost, and (2) there is a great need for workers. They need to be challenged to consider if they are the answer to Jesus's prayer to take the gospel to the ends of the earth. It is possible that the missionaries who will take the gospel to the unreached and unengaged people groups are sitting in your youth group each week.

If you have students who feel called to missions, connect them with gospel-centered mission organizations, like the International Mission Board (imb.org). Send them to get theological training at solid Christian colleges and seminaries like Spurgeon College (spurgeoncollege.com). Spurgeon College even has a program called "Fusion" that allows students to pursue their degree while engaging in international missions (http://spurgeoncollege.com/academics/fusion/).

In short, student ministries should challenge students to consider becoming missionaries and help those who are called to missions connect with solid organizations and institutions to train them and launch them into service.

Conclusion

Our world desperately needs to hear the gospel of Jesus Christ. There are approximately 7.6 billion people on the planet at the time of my writing. Many of them have never heard the name Jesus. Apart from the gospel, they will spend eternity separated from God. This must change. Student ministries can play a role in changing the landscape by raising up a generation of students who are committed to the gospel and the Great Commission. Let's train students to share the gospel. Let's take students on mission trips to tell unbelievers about Jesus Christ. Let's challenge students to surrender to mission work. And let's watch God use students to change the world.

CHAPTER 8

STUDENT MINISTRY, THE BIBLE, AND PARENTS

Rechab Gray

Article VIII: A healthy student ministry elevates the parent's role as primary discipler over the helpful but secondary roles of the student pastor and volunteers.

Students are Leaving the Church Because Their Parents Already Left

I was on Temple University's campus when I met Will. Will was an African-American who happened to be studying engineering. I recently graduated from the same program, so I sought to build on that commonality in order to share the gospel with him. When I asked him if he saw himself as a Christian, he explained in no uncertain terms that he was a proud atheist.

Now, among African-Americans, I do not normally meet self-proclaimed atheists. Most of the time they maintain some loose religious affiliation or consider themselves "spiritual." Will was not only rare because he identified with atheism but also because he was raised that way, his father and mother having trained him with rebuttals against Christians in particular.

Though Will was an anomaly back in 2012, I meet more and more young black men who don't simply disbelieve the gospel but were raised to do so. What has happened in the past few decades that has caused so many young men to reject Jesus and his church?

I believe it comes down to two primary issues: the church's absence in the life of students, and the father's absence in the life of the church.

Youth Leaders Thought They Could Replace Parents

God set up the family structure with a father and mother in mind, a pattern reinforced in the New Testament. Church leaders themselves are judged by this standard (1 Tim 3:2–5). Yet, at some point, student leaders began thinking they could own the position that has been divinely ordained by God himself—namely, the role of primary disciple maker in the life of the child or teenager. And I wouldn't blame them. Many parents see student ministry as a glorified version of day care: a way to not only watch their kids but allow them to have fun and learn in the process. This is great! But when the expectation for a student pastor begins to shift from being a partner to being a parent, everyone is in dangerous territory.

I fell into often in north Philadelphia. Our student ministry was made up of about thirty young men who were not church members. Most of them were professing Muslims. Along with the weekly challenge of explaining to them that it was okay to read along with us in the Bible even though they were Muslim, we also had the difficulty of making sure they arrived home safely, as many of them were lived in difficult conditions. These were bright, well-behaved, respectful, and hilarious young dudes. They loved to laugh and learn. They had no business being in a church on a Friday night, and yet they kept coming. One mother, a Muslim, finally told us why she allowed her son to come on Fridays: she knew he was safe and well cared for. This was encouraging but also sad.

Knowing the difficulty many of them were facing caused me to take on a savior mentality. But I knew Friday just wasn't enough. Where would they go if they needed a safe place Sunday through Thursday? If I wasn't going to share the gospel with them, who would? I began to bite off more than I could chew, and pretty soon I had very little margin in my life. Then it hit me: All the time I was spending pre-discipling these young men, I could be spending pouring into their parents and guardians, whose impact on their lives would be far greater than mine ever could be.

I finally understood that though I was called to help grow the students entrusted to my care, my role would always be that of a deputy, not a director. If I wanted to see real change occur, I needed to turn at least some of my attention to parents. They were designed to be the long-term instruments of change in the lives of their teenagers. I knew if I could see parents come to Christ, then the impact they could make in the life of their child would skyrocket. This should teach us something about how student pastors ought to think of their role. And though it fed my ego to think I could rescue all of these young men, my ego needed to go hungry in order to see real growth happen. This begins with expectations—proper expectations the parent can have of pastors and proper expectations that we have of the parents. Every situation is different, and inner-city issues call for inner-city solutions, but that solution is always built upon the foundation of Christ, his word, and his design.

Student Ministry is a Church-Based, Family Ministry

Youth ministry is family ministry. In the book of Exodus God uses Moses to powerfully deliver the people of Israel from bondage and oppression. God rescues them through many signs and wonders. After the true "mission impossible" is accomplished, God gives them ten commands to follow—all but two of which come with grave consequences. After he wraps up the first four commandments, which are all about their direct devotion to God, the very next commandment turns toward the children, "Honor your father and your mother" (Exod 20:12). God could have placed any commandment immediately after these primary four, but he directed the people's attention toward the family.

Later in the Pentateuch the *Shema* is proclaimed, "Hear, O Israel: The LORD our God, the LORD is one" (Deut 6:4). The Lord makes sure his people understand the preeminent place reserved for the Lord alone. And right after *Shema*, this most important announcement, attention is placed again on the family. This time the spotlight is on the parents, and the call is for fathers and mothers to teach the commandments to their children.

If you place these two texts together you have this formula: worship God, honor your parents, disciple your children. If these three are occurring, the Israelites are set up for success.

So, what happened? Judges 2:10 tells us, "There arose another generation after them who did not know the Lord or the work that he had done for Israel." Often this has been taught to mean that the parents of the former generation didn't teach their children. This is absolutely true. But discipleship is a two-way street. The children also might have been stubbornly refusing to hear the instruction being given. Ultimately, the family structure in Israel needed revamping, retooling, and restoration.

This is exactly what Malachi prophesies will occur during the coming day of the Lord when the Messiah arrives. The last inspired words penned in the Old Testament, the words appearing on the sacred page right before the eternal King becomes an incarnated, divine embryo are these:

> *Behold I will send you Elijah the prophet before the great and awesome day of the Lord comes. And he will turn the hearts of fathers to their children and the hearts of children to their fathers, lest I come and strike the land with a decree of utter destruction.* (Mal 4:5–6)

Do you see the importance of fathers in your student ministry? It is one of the signs of the arrival of the new kingdom that fathers and children will be in sync (even Justin Timberlake and his dad). If this were not to occur, a declaration of destruction would take its place. Involve fathers in student ministry. Where relationships are broken between a son and a father, fight to see them restored.

Where a mother has no hope for her rebellious son, advocate on behalf of the mother and exhort her son to be respectful. Call the parents to raise their children and call the children to respect their parents. Be a mediator if you have to. Take care not to be forceful or thoughtless in inserting yourself as a wedge between families, but where the Spirit gives room, help them both to see the reconciling power of Christ! Why? Because the dominant influence in that student's life will most likely not be you, but the parents. This is God's awesome arrangement! Let us adhere to it with joy in all situations and see the fruit of his plan flourish!

Next Steps

As a Student Pastor, You are More Like an Uncle or Aunt than a Cousin

I used to love going to my older cousins' house. They let me do things I could never do at home. But when their dad came around, it was different. I'd still get more freedom than I did at home, but I knew that if I acted out, my father would be informed.

This is because my uncle was a brother to my father long before he was an uncle to me. He cared deeply for me and knew that discipline by my parents was best for me and was ultimately rooted in love.

Too often we see ourselves as cousins or friends with the students under our care. This can create a chasm between us and as parents. That's the last thing you want. It is divisive to our relationship with their parents and detrimental to their own growth. *When a solution isn't apparent, side with a parent!*

Pursue Partnership with the Parents

Notice I didn't say relationship. Some parents won't be ecstatic about being buddy-buddy with the student pastor. Many will. But virtually all parents will want someone who is partnering with them to see their child flourish. Ask this question of at least one guardian of every student who attends your ministry: "How can I serve you and be a blessing to (Student Name)?" This question clarifies your role as a helper who comes alongside the parent and their role as a parent.

Design Events and Programs That Welcome Parental Involvement

As a student pastor, I absolutely loved retreats. However, I have learned that banquets and family days have been even more impactful. At banquets and family days, I am able to meet and dialogue with the parents who have great influence on the students I am pouring into. Make these a regular part of your yearly schedule.

Conclusion

Eventually, we must grasp the fact that the discipleship of students is the work of God himself. However, he has designed that dads and moms should play the most prominent human role in that work. That is the biblical ideal. The faster we understand that, the faster we can begin the synergetic work of compounding discipleship at home with the discipleship at church. God has equipped you not only to raise up a generation of students but of parents as well, who in tandem will do extensive damage to the kingdom of darkness.

CHAPTER 9

STUDENT MINISTRY, THE BIBLE, AND MULTI-ETHNICITY

Joel Muddamalle

Article IX: A healthy student ministry pursues ethnic diversity as displayed in the book of Revelation over contentment with a monochromatic ministry.

I've always loved working with students, and truth be told, I think once a "student-ministry guy" always a "student-ministry guy." My wife and I were part of a new church plant in Roseville, California, with an eclectic group of students. Many of them hung out at youth group but didn't run in the same circles at school. My wife and I planned a get-together at our house to connect with these students, and even more importantly, to provide an opportunity for them to connect to each other.

I thought hard about how to start our time together—something fun, memorable, surprising! So, my wife and I created a game called "name that ingredient." We split the students into two teams. Each team had five minutes to raid our pantry to try and find five of the most unique ingredients. The other team would have to taste the ingredients blindfolded and try to guess the different ingredients.

You should know that I'm Indian (like from India), and my wife is white (like from Vancouver, Washington). The students were shocked when they came across ingredients they had never seen or heard of. They chose ingredients like curry leaves, cardamom, turmeric powder, and some very special homemade chili powder my grandmother sent me from India.

What happened next was not part of my plan or strategy for the night. I don't think I even opened up my notes for the small devotion I planned on sharing. The conversation over the next two hours (with parents honking horns outside because we went way over our time!) was a marked moment in my life and the lives of those students. In that room were students from different backgrounds, cultures, and ethnicities. Many of them had never interacted with or even knew much about Indian culture and food. They asked questions about India and its culture. Then, surprisingly, they shared their stories and backgrounds, the impact of their ethnicity in their lives, schools, friendships, and church.

That night, different and very diverse people were uniquely knit together through honest conversation, some vulnerability, and a shared experience. My wife and I didn't realize it then, but a family started to form—a family of multi-ethnic students from diverse cultural backgrounds who found unity in Christ. Those students realized that the things their culture told them should separate and divide were the means by which they could and should be united in the gospel.

Conversations about ethnicity and cultural differences can be volatile. It is sensitive and challenging; however, our culture is not backing down from this topic that we often avoid. e may not call it avoidance. We say we are choosing to focus on the things that unite us, and ethnicity and cultural differences are volatile topics best avoided. This seems to produce homogenous student ministries. In other words, by avoiding the problem and the fundamental challenges that are associated with it, we are creating more-divided environments.

Scripture tells a story of unity. As my pastor Dr. Derwin Gray says, it's not about being color blind but realizing that humanity is color blessed. It is not a homogenous covenant people of God but a glorious multi-ethnic family of God that was first promised to Abraham and realized in the formation of the church at Pentecost. Scripture attests throughout to the formation of a multi-ethnic covenant family of God that was promised to Abraham in the Old Testament (Gen 12:3), made possible by Jesus in his victory over sin and death (1 Cor 15:56–57; Col 2:15), realized in the formation of the church at Pentecost (Acts 2), and modeled in perfection in the Trinity—unified diversity. Thus, our student ministries should reflect the beauty of a multi-ethnic family.

The Pursuit and Purpose of a Multi-Ethnic Student Ministry

We may avoid talking about ethnicity and culture, and we may think the development of diversity in our student ministries will happen "organically." This is just not the case. You and I are called to make disciples of "all nations" (Matt 28:19). This is something that we must pursue and seek after first because it is the anticipated promise of the Old Testament. We find the clearest indication of this from the apostle Paul in Galatians. In Galatians 3:7 Paul identifies the origins of the formation of this multi-ethnic family rooted in the Abrahamic covenant. For Paul, a multi-ethnic family was at the very heart of the Abrahamic covenant. The Abrahamic covenant found in Genesis 12:3 anticipates a specific multi-ethnic destiny for humanity and the church because all humanity is made in the image and likeness of God (Gen 1:27). In Galatians 2 and 3 Paul articulates the reality that God is fulfilling the covenant promise he made to Abraham by creating a single multi-ethnic family. So, as we are pursuing the formation of multi-ethnic student ministries filled with diversity, we join the journey of the fulfillment of this covenant promise.

The monumental event at Pentecost was the establishment of the church, which is first identified as a multi-ethnic community (Acts 2:1–13). Ethnic diversity is made explicit by naming the represented nationalities at Pentecost. the list of nations sweeps from the eastern part of the

Roman world and runs all the way to the west. It begins in what is present-day Iran (Parthia) and includes all the territories east of the Euphrates River. Pentecost reversed Babel (Gen 11:1–9), where humanity was first divided as judgment for human wickedness. However, Pentecost reverses that judgment through the Spirit, who gives a common language for a diverse people.

The goal is unity in diversity, not unity *absent* diversity. Possibly the most convicting reason to pursue this unity is found in the fundamental relationship among the Godhead. In as much as the Trinity is divinely diverse, it is truly unified. So how is this unity achieved? Through the reciprocal self-dedication among the Trinity. Self-sacrificing love undergirds divine unity. Further, it serves as a roadmap for how the church must pursue unity in its diversity. This is the key for a unified yet diverse multi-ethnic student ministry.

Our student ministries are empowered by the Spirit and commissioned to share the good news of the gospel. Charles Spurgeon reminds us of the ancient goodness of the gospel: "The true gospel is no new thing; it is as old as the hills. It was heard in Eden before man was driven from the garden, and it has since been repeated in sundry ways and diverse places, even to this day."[9] The good news of the gospel unites people from different backgrounds into a diverse, multi-ethnic family of God.

The same tensions present during the time of Paul exist today in the halls of the schools, within homes, and even within churches. The same ethnic, social, and generational conflicts have caused immense pain and trauma to individuals. The hurt is real, and the result in our modern ministry context is separation and division that is anything but what God intended for the church. For these reasons, we must recognize the need for diversity within our student ministries not merely because it is a positive step forward sociologically for our communities; but we must do so because it is what Scripture anticipates in the Old Testament. Christ's death, burial, and resurrection make this possible, and this is what the Spirit of God formed in Acts 2. We must build diverse, multi-ethnic student ministries at every level.

We have to fight the urge to create student ministries that are homogenous and therefore bring uniformity. Honestly, doing that is probably the fast track to exponential growth. However, it's not what Scripture calls us to. Paul reminds the Corinthian church that unity is not uniformity but unity in diversity (1 Cor 12:12–27). In other words, the expression of diversity does not and should not obliterate unity but is a glorious expression of it.

The Next Steps

At this point, things may feel daunting. Seeing the importance and the biblical mandate for a church and student ministry that reflects the multi-ethnic family of God should move us toward action and implementation. However, where do we start? The next steps to building a biblically faithful student ministry that reflects the multi-ethnic family of God requires us to live from a conviction of what we know is right. Go toward that truth through our actions. Moreover, never stop growing in our spiritual maturity.

The unity achieved (and fought for) in the first-century church was a result of the formation of intentional multi-ethnic church communities that were more than merely a gathering of like-minded people but were a fellowship of family members united by the divine blood of Christ. Our student ministries today must follow the example of the Lord by pursuing unity in the midst of diversity.

As student ministries pursue unity in the midst of diversity, it serves as a missional witness to a broken world longing for the unity that can only be achieved through Christ and by the power of the Spirit. This type of unity and peace is the desperate cry of our students' generation that can be seen through their activity in a variety of social justice movements. The only true and final movement that could achieve this indeed is the movement of Jesus and his church.

Prayerfully pursue the following steps.[10]

Commit to Prayer

Possibly one of the most overlooked yet vital components of the life of the believer is prayer. Pray for the Lord to bring students to your ministry who reflect your cultural and demographic context. Pray for open hearts and minds of students and leaders. Plead for unity in the midst of diversity. Through prayer, we commune with the Father, seeking his wisdom and discernment as we try to build biblically faithful student ministries empowered by the Spirit that bring honor to the Son.

Invite Potential Leaders/Students from Different Ethnic and Cultural Backgrounds over for Dinner or Coffee

The pursuit of a biblically faithful, multi-ethnic student ministry begins on the foundation of relationship and trust. Commit to sincere and genuine relationships with people of different ethnicities. As you invite them into your story, pray the Spirit of God would allow you to be invited into their stories. If you are a minority and leading, bring that out! One of our favorite things to do with new friends is Indian dinner night. The ancient tradition of food and fellowship often has the capacity to produce authentic relationships.

Embrace and Celebrate Cultural Difference and Ethnicities

Be aware of cultural and ethnic holidays. Take time to celebrate these moments. Learn about them and leverage these opportunities to engage with your students to share from their experiences. This builds a culture that celebrates diversity, which is an ingredient in the development of unity.

Be Intentional in Developing a Leadership Team That Is Diverse in Gender, Age, and Ethnicity

Throughout the Gospels we find Jesus calling his disciples to the work of ministry (e.g., Matt 4:18–21; Mark 8:34–35). Be on the lookout for those that have a heart and passion but are waiting for an invitation. One of the most important means of building a multi-ethnic student ministry is when your student leadership is reflective of the desired outcome.

Create Safe Spaces for Honest Conversation and Dialogue

Fair warning: this is not easy. At every turn we will be tempted to hit the abort button. Don't do it! When we are faced with those difficult situations and circumstances that threaten the very fabric of our unity, lean in! Create safe spaces for dialogue and discussion. These spaces have the capacity for student ministries to realize and bear the fruit of relationships that have been rooted in and formed by Christ. These spaces can become places where students experience the tremendous grace of the gospel.

The multi-ethnic family is itself not the final goal. The real fruit comes from the overflow of relational community with a multi-ethnic and diverse context. In other words, God's sanctifying process is at work through the Spirit in the midst of this diverse community. Multi-ethnic student ministries provide a way forward for students who find themselves in a culture damaged by sinful racism and prejudice. The local church and specifically student ministries within the church today must pursue this vision of a multi-ethnic family because it is not only described and prescribed in Scripture but even more so because unity in diversity is modeled in the Trinity. We must become one as God the Father, God the Son, and God the Holy Spirit are one. Our oneness is modeled to the world through our unity. The unity found in the midst of a diverse multi-ethnic student ministry will serve as a missional witness to the world at large of the goodness of the Gospel of Jesus.

Recommended Resources

Brown, Leon, ed. *All Are Welcome: Toward a Multi-Everything Church.* Oklahoma City: Storied Publishing, 2018.

Emerson, Michael and Christian Smith. *Divided by Faith*. Oxford: Oxford University Press, 2000.

Gray, Derwin L. *The High-Definition Leader: Building Multiethnic Churches in a Multiethnic World*. Nashville: Thomas Nelson, 2015.

Rah, Soong-Chan. *The Next Evangelicalism: Freeing the Church from Western Cultural Captivity*. Downers Grove, IL: IVP, 2009.

CHAPTER 10

STUDENT MINISTRY, THE BIBLE, AND EVANGELISM

Joel Cowart

Article X: A healthy student ministry values training and mobilizing students to join the whole body in sharing the gospel over assuming students will naturally share the gospel on their own.

Duty Over Gifting

I met a guy during my college years who was about as far away from being a Christian as anyone could be. He was committed to being offensive to just about everyone he met (he pushed people away for the sheer fun of it!). Somehow, in the providence of God, he and I became friends. I recognized how special this was because he didn't have many friends. I took an interest in everything he enjoyed, and to this day I recognize his influence in my life in the video games I enjoy and how I view the world. After a few months he agreed to study the Bible with me. By the end of the semester, he confessed Christ as Lord and was soon baptized. THAT WAS CAUSE FOR CELEBRATION, so we threw a party!

These types of stories are few and far between. In the American church, evangelism has really taken on a personality of its own—and not a good personality. It's all about finding those who are the most outgoing people, those God has specifically gifted as "evangelists," and working with them to perfect their technique so that they can make us feel like our church is growing and cares about the lost. Furthermore, in our increasingly self-centered world, evangelism has become less about a burden for hell-bound sinners or a passion for sharing the gospel of our Lord Jesus Christ and more about how uncomfortable evangelism makes us feel. This is a tragedy. American Christians, by and large, don't want to break out of our comfort zone. If it doesn't come naturally, it's not our gifting, so we feel we don't have to do it. But as H. B. Charles, Jr. has said, "The Bible doesn't emphasize the gift of evangelism. It emphasizes the duty."[11]

Evangelism has died a slow death in our churches. It has died because we have psyched ourselves out by getting caught up in questions of method or gifting. It has died when we think our way out of it by falling to evangelistic phobias and self-centeredness. Evangelism dies when we schedule our way out of it. We have been very creative in finding excuses to avoid evangelism, even though one is usually enough. In short, evangelism in the North American church dies because we have condemned the duty to the bottom of the church's priority list.

Our self-centered approaches to evangelism allow us to justify overlooking it altogether. We blow right past Christ's command to evangelize (Matt 28:19). Evangelism is a duty, student pastor! And a glorious one. Instead of recognizing this duty, we emphasize evangelistic giftedness (Eph 4:11) that we have conveniently defined so as to give ourselves a pass. The truth is we need to put all of our excuses aside and rekindle the simplicity of a burning passion to share Christ. As a student pastor, it's especially important that you embody this passion because Christ is using you to grow his church. You are teaching the younger members of your church what to value. Likewise, your youth workers who lead small groups, oversee events, and do one-on-one discipling are watching and imitating you. They will catch what flows from your heart more than what flows from your mouth. You lead the way, and a true passion for evangelism must exist in our ministries and in our lives if we ever hope to reach the youth of our cities with the gospel.

Cultivating an Urgency to Share

Matthew 9:35–38 says,

> Jesus continued going around to all the towns and villages, teaching in their synagogues, preaching the good news of the kingdom, and healing every disease and every sickness. When he saw the crowds, he felt compassion for them, because they were distressed and dejected, like sheep without a shepherd. Then he said to his disciples, "The harvest is abundant, but the workers are few. Therefore, pray to the Lord of the harvest to send out workers into his harvest."

There's a certain urgency this passage shows us. Matthew writes that Jesus traveled "to all the towns and villages." He didn't skip a single town or village. What was so important for Jesus to not miss a single town or village? "The good news [the Gospel] of the kingdom" with everyone. He taught it in their places of worship. He heralded this gospel everywhere he went. He demonstrated its power over all of creation. Jesus appealed to the people to trust in him, and his appeal was urgent.

Jesus walked around with a broken heart because everywhere he looked he saw people who were distressed and dejected and felt compassion for them. Jesus saw people; and he wasn't politically correct when he saw them. They were damaged, deserted, and destitute, and he didn't pretend that they were better off without him. Jesus's heart was broken for these people and their condition, which propelled him into the state of urgency seen in the Gospels. Jesus went to them in every place because he understood that they were lost and needed help.

We stray! We need help! We are sheep in need of a shepherd. The beauty of this metaphor is that sheep are so dumb and defenseless that they basically need someone to think for them. The needed a protector, a shepherd. It is a pastoral concern. It was Moses's concern before he died,

> May the Lord, the God who gives breath to all, appoint a man over the community who will go out before them and come back in before them, and who will bring them out and bring them in, so that the Lord's community won't be like sheep without a shepherd. (Num 27:16–17)

Moses's fear for the people was realized several times throughout the Old Testament. By the time Jesus came on the scene, the people had been lost and wandering for centuries. Hence, Jesus met them with compassion and urgency. It's easy to read these stories and think to ourselves, "I know people who are lost." But, the truth is, we are reading about ourselves: "We all went astray like sheep; we all have turned to our own way; and the Lord has punished [Jesus] for the iniquity of us all" (Isa 53:6).

Isaiah makes it even more personal. We are the dumb sheep our Lord rescued. What a gift! Thank you, Jesus! I needed to be rescued. I had gone my own way. Christ paid my debt and brought me into the sheepfold. This is the gospel—Jesus had compassion and urgency to rescue rebel sinners while we were still rebel sinners.

This God-Man, Christ Jesus, came to identify with us so that He could save us (Heb. 4:15). In His identifying, His urgency, His broken-heartedness, Jesus teaches us that everyone needs to hear the Gospel of Jesus Christ. The fields are ripe for harvest (Jn. 4:35-38). At the same time, there are not enough workers sharing this good news. There aren't enough shepherds bringing the people out and bringing the people in (Nu. 27:17). John 4:35-38 shows us that we need student pastors to be passionate about the gospel and showing the way.

Jesus commands us to "pray to the Lord of the harvest" (Matt 9:38). This is not your average command to pray. The Greek word here, *deomai*, is only used this once by Matthew and most often used by Luke (e.g., Luke 5:12, the leper falling facedown before Jesus "begged him" [*deomai*] to make him clean). *Deomai* communicates begging "for something that is indispensable or necessary."[12] Jesus is commanding us to beg him for workers. We need a sense of urgency. We need to regularly pray to God, begging him for this absolutely vital thing to happen—that people would share the gospel with the lost and the lost would be saved and added to the church! Here is Jesus declaring the urgency of the matter. On the other side of this passage, the Matthew 10 records Jesus commissioning his apostles to be the answer to this urgent prayer that he commanded them to pray. It's funny how Christ gives his followers a passion and then equips them to fulfill their Christ-centered passion. And you are never more serious about a thing than when you pray about it. And the degree to which you pray about it is the degree to which you are serious about it. "Pray to the Lord of the harvest to send out workers into his harvest." Every blood-bought church member in your pews is there because someone shared the good news with them!

Taking Steps

At the age of five, I worshiped the ground my daddy walked on. I hung on to his every word and tried to do everything I saw him do. So, when he taught me to evangelize by passing out these little pieces of paper that had information about Jesus on them (tracts for the old cats out there who know what I'm talking about), man, this short little chunky kid couldn't wait to evangelize. It helped that we lived on the same street as the local high school and all the teenagers had to walk past my house to go home after school. I would stand out on the sidewalk with my big fat cheeks, smiling ear to ear, just hoping they would be willing to take my piece of paper. In my mind, I was the greatest evangelist ever because I could do exactly what my daddy taught me to do. I was the best at smiling and handing out this piece of paper. I was a great evangelist! And my daddy was a great teacher because at the age of five I was able to reproduce what he taught me! What did a five-year-old kid know about evangelism? Nothing. But I did it because my daddy taught me how important and how simple it was. He even let me do it with him so that I was confident that I could do it without him. What my dad and I were doing was by no means flawless, but we were eager, and my dad was patiently modeling faithful evangelism to me.

What are we teaching and modeling for our students in the way of evangelism? Are we communicating the proper passion and urgency, or are we showing that it's a back-burner issue? Do we teach them to share their faith? Do we celebrate new believers? Do we throw parties for baptisms (figuratively or literally)?

Student pastors do not have to be evangelism experts. They don't even have to personally train every single student to do evangelism. But they must engage the opportunities for evangelism that God has already placed around them. If your church has an evangelism ministry, talk to the leader about training your students when the evangelism ministry is already going out to evangelize, and then take your students with them.

> For I passed on to you as most important what I also received: that Christ died for our sins according to the Scriptures, that he was buried, that he was raised on the third day according to the Scripture. (1 Cor 15:3–4)

Calm fears by telling your students they don't have to say anything new. The most important parts of the gospel they can repeat from what they've heard. Tell your students to share a basic gospel message: "Jesus lived a perfect life. He died in the place of sinners. He was buried, and on the third day he rose from the grave to give us new life. When a person repents of their sin and places their whole life and trust in Jesus, making him Lord, they are saved from God's anger and hell." Finally, affirm them! Tell them somebody will say yes to Jesus. They said yes, and so did their peers in the student ministry. God isn't finished yet.

Next Steps

Protect the sense of urgency.

Protect the sense of urgency! Preach passion and compassion for the lost. Fight to get your kids across the evangelistic finish line so they can say, "I shared Christ with someone today!" Celebrate that!

Be church focused, not youth focused.

If there are already ministries doing evangelism work in your church, partner with them. Students should be the evangelistic labor force of the local church. Use those evangelistic types in your church to train and deploy your students.

Plan evangelistic events.

Have an "each one reach one" youth service once a quarter, or once a month. This is a concerted effort where each student seeks to bring one friend who is not a member of a church.

Pray.

Prayer signifies importance. When you start praying, you mean business. If you want to see God work through your ministry for evangelism, pray. Do the work of evangelism. It's one thing to train for evangelism. It's another thing to do evangelism. Schedule evangelism outings on the same day or shortly after a training.

ENDNOTES

1. Steven C. Roy, *What God Thinks When We Fail* (Downers Grove: IVP Books, 2011), 11-12.
2. Tweet from Dr. Steven J. Lawson. @DrStevenJLawson. https://twitter.com/DrStevenJLawson/status/567147719685177345.
3. Brian Payne, Jim Orrick, and Ryan Fullerton, *Encountering God through Expository Preaching: Connecting God's People to God's Presence through God's Word* (B&H Academic, 2017), XV.
4. Dave Wright "A Brief History of Student Ministry," The Gospel Coalition, April 2, 2012, www.thegospelcoalition.org/article/a-brief-history-of-student-ministry/.
5. Purity culture refers to the now recognizable and pervasive mindset, typically accompanied by a few extrabiblical customs (True Love Waits, promise rings, courtship, courtship literature, etc.), which often prescribes rigid and potentially legalistic parameters in order to preserve unsullied sexual purity. To be clear, I am not saying that the Bible does not hold up sexual virginity as the ideal. It does! However, regardless of the sexual state Christ finds a person,

forgiveness, hope for future wholeness, and sexual holiness is theirs the moment they repent and believe.

6. Aspects of this section are were drawn from, similar too, and inspired by a blog post I wrote for FTC.co entitled "Sex: The Cathedral of Our Culture," published April 5, 2017.
7. Aspects of this section are drawn from, similar too, and inspired by a blog post I wrote for FTC.co entitled "8 Books that Have Influenced Me," published January 11, 2017.
8. J. I. Packer, *Evangelism and the Sovereignty of God* (Downers Grove, IL: IVP, 2012); and Greg Gilbert, *What is the Gospel?* (Wheaton, IL: Crossway, 2010).
9. Charles Spurgeon, *Galatians*, ed. Elliot Ritzema, Spurgeon Commentary Series (Bellingham, WA: Lexham, 2013), Galatians 3:8.
10. I'm grateful to J. Scott Samarco (student ministry pastor at Transformation Church) for his help in processing and developing these applicable next steps. He has faithfully modeled and developed these principles effectively in the student ministry culture at Transformation Church, and we have seen the beauty of a multi-ethnic church and student ministry.
11. Quote by: H.B. Charles, Jr. Date: 4/21/18 Location: Shiloh Church, Jacksonville, FL Talk Title: Shiloh Seminar: Evangelism.

12. Faithlife Corporation. (2019). to beg (need) (Version 7.19) [Computer software]. *Logos Bible Software Bible Sense Lexicon*. Bellingham, WA: Faithlife Corporation. Retrieved from https://ref.ly/logos4/Senses?KeyId=ws.beg+need.v.01

Made in the USA
Columbia, SC
28 January 2020